PACE COLLEGE
OPPORTVNITAS
ARS COMMERCIVM CIVITAS
MCMVI
NEW YORK

D1214561

# 1918

## YEAR OF CRISIS, YEAR OF CHANGE

*Books by Joseph Carter*

A HISTORY OF THE FRENCH CONSTITUTION
A HAGIOGRAPHY OF ITALIAN RENAISSANCE PAINTING
HISTORY OF THE 14TH ARMORED DIVISION
DEATH AND FOUR LOVERS (a novel)

# 1918

## YEAR OF CRISIS, YEAR OF CHANGE

•

JOSEPH CARTER

Prentice-Hall, Inc., Englewood Cliffs, New Jersey

*1918: Year of Crisis, Year of Change*
by Joseph Carter

Library of Congress Catalog Card Number: 68–56622
Printed in the United States of America • *T*
Prentice-Hall International, Inc., *London*
Prentice-Hall of Australia, Pty. Ltd., *Sydney*
Prentice-Hall of Canada, Ltd., *Toronto*
Prentice-Hall of India Private Ltd., *New Delhi*
Prentice-Hall of Japan, Inc., *Tokyo*

FOR

*Alison*

# INTRODUCTION

The year 1918 marks the beginning of the world of today. Through such trivial and mundane accessories of current living as the factory-made cigarette, the wristwatch, the flashlight, the safety razor—all of them hardly more than curiosities before World War I—the new shape of living can be seen emerging, congenitally twisted by four years of the world's most terrible war and the frenetic pace of life on the home front. In the United States, there came prohibition; throughout the western world there came the emancipation of women. A new sort of hero was born. Earlier wars had celebrated the foot soldier as the hero of battles, but from World War I emerged the pursuit pilot, above all others—the shining knight of combat—the airplane itself as the most glorious of all possible weapons.

Already in 1918 commonplaces of today's living were becoming apparent. The first of the mass small-home developments were a-building. The first of the heavy-density highways—forerunners of today's six-to-twelve-lane giants—were being constructed. The telephone and the automobile, former oddities that evoked feature stories in the Sunday newspapers, were becoming staples in ordinary households across the nation.

If there were any observers then who foresaw the magnitude of the change that the technological revolution would bring to the world, beyond an occasional fiction writer, the world as a whole paid them little attention. Nor is it possible to measure the impetus given to this change by World War I. It may be argued, for example, that the basic thrust for mass production—or, more properly, the interchangeable part that is the keystone of mass production—came from the insatiable need for armaments that the automatic weapons of the war created. How much the use of aircraft in the war stimulated the growth of the aircraft industry as a whole is a matter of debate, but there is little doubt that the use of the truck as a vehicle of mass transportation had its beginnings in the war. A shelled-out railroad line carrying war materials might take days or even weeks before the roadbed could be rebuilt and the tracks relaid; a shelled-out truck route could be rebuilt in hours with rock taken from the adjoining fields.

The technological revolution aside, however, there is no doubt at all about the vast and interlocking—and frequently contradictory—changes that the first world war brought to the world of today. The first and, still to this moment perhaps, the most important was the destruction of so many of the great empires and the dynasties, the systems by which so much of the world had been governed for so long. The destruction of these political institutions produced gaps in the power structure at the same time that gaps appeared in the postwar economics of nations—not alone those defeated and despoiled—which were to plunge the world into the most disastrous depression it had ever known. Often the vacuum created by these circumstances would be filled effectively only by the dictators who later emerged. It is hard to conceive of a Hitler coming to power in a Germany where the Hohenzollerns still ruled, or of a Mussolini exercising supreme authority in an Italy where even as weak a monarch as Umberto headed a prosperous state.

World War I, too, began the downfall of the modern middle class Protestant ethic of the western world—an ethic that, based firmly on the morality of the dollar, puts on the middle class the onus of maintaining those standards of behavior deemed most acceptable for preserving the social fabric. A re-reading of the Ten Commandments and of the admonishments of Ben Franklin cover most of these standards. It is the nature of all wars to destroy the world-as-it-is to a greater or lesser degree, but the length of World War I and the magnitude of its slaughter, accompanied by revolution, starvation, and pestilence, and followed shortly by an enormous economic depression, all combined to erode the ordinary man's trust in the shape of things as they were. It is here that some thinkers find the beginning of the "God is dead" philosophy current in the world today; and democracy, that venerable and war-weary God of political creation suffered the indignity of being challenged by new totalitarian deities.

A look back at the year 1918, with the advantage of fifty years of hindsight, reveals it as a year when the shape of today's world can be quite clearly discerned. The years before are too beclouded by the smoke of war; in the years afterward the changes were already under way. It is possible, of course, to read too much into the past. If it is agreed that the real problems of the world today are the threat of nuclear war, the explosion of population, and the pollution of the earth, how many of them may be discerned fifty years ago? Not pollution, certainly, although most assuredly it was present. Population? Well, the fact that the population of the world was 1,819,000,000 in 1920, after some 50 million had been slain in the previous six years—an increase of 231 million over 1910—might indicate that population sooner or later would have to become a problem. And as for nuclear war, there are those today who argue that nuclear weapons never again will be used, just as poison gas has not been used since World War I, presumably on the premise that each side has the capability of annihilating the other.

The world fifty years from now is being shaped by the forces at work today, and conceivably we may read our own lives in the stars of 1918.

# CONTENTS

# I

## ARMISTICE

No war, or battle's sound
Was heard the world around
The idle spear and shield
Were high up hung.

MILTON

THE WINTER OF THE world was ending. November 11, 1918, could not be anything except a day of transcendent joy. The most savage war the world had ever known had come to an end. It was early morning for the western world when the official announcement was made. A gray, cold, misty morning. It was 6:50 in the morning when the British General Headquarters sent the message to inform its armies that hostilities would cease at 11:00 A.M.; it was 2:45 A.M. in Washington when the State Department issued its formal announcement to a sleeping nation that the war was over. Eight minutes later in New York, the first silent sign of peace was seen: the Statue of Liberty in New York harbor was lit by searchlights.

As the dawn approached in New York, trumpets of victory and of joy began to sound, faintly at first, then louder and more loudly until they filled the air. Down at the Battery the sound of bugles was first heard, then sirens began to scream, and the noise of victory swept upward. In Times Square, a tall, fresh-cheeked English girl "with the bloom of Devonshire still on her cheeks," according to one eyewitness, climbed to the exterior platform of Liberty Hall, a temporary, wartime, one-story building used for innumerable rallies and patriotic speeches in the triangle formed by the intersection of Broadway with Seventh Avenue. The girl held up her hand for silence.

In a clear and silvery voice, she sang the doxology—"Praise God from Whom All Blessings Flow," and for that moment an almost churchly silence fell over Times Square; hats came off and heads were bowed. As she finished, the roar of sound began again.

This was not New York's first armistice celebration. Four days earlier, on Thursday, November 7, there had been the celebrated "False Armistice," a piece of journalistic enterprise that had earned United Press a number of critics. The premature wire service announcing an end of hostilities had arrived in New York shortly after noon that day, and Mayor John F. Hylan had immediately proclaimed a holiday, but the jubilation had hardly begun when word came that the news dispatch was wrong.

Now on November 11, even from the first, there was no doubt but that this time the war was really over. Newsboys were again hawking extras, but Hylan had no need to proclaim a holiday. The city made a bluff at working in the beginning hours of the morning, but by noon the bluff had been given up. Crying, laughing, kissing, hugging, ringing bells and tooting horns, people poured into the streets. By midafternoon an estimated million people were jammed onto Broadway. The *Evening World* concluded that "it is quite possible that never in history anywhere has there been so diversified an exhibition of joy."

As the earth rotated westward the celebrations of Armistice Day spread across the nation, but the crowds were biggest in New York. Alongside the as-many-as-possible of the city's six million population were the soldiers and sailors visiting or stationed there, factory workers from as far away as Stamford and Bridgeport, longshoremen from the docks, workers from the Brooklyn Navy Yard, crews of foreign ships in port. Girls in coveys of twenty to fifty swooped down on any male in uniform to kiss him. The city's schools and factories and shops were shut down. In the Wall Street area, 155 tons of paper (the Sanitation Department guessed later) were showered down from the windows of the skyscrapers. The mayor tried to lead an impromptu parade of city employees uptown from City Hall, but the crowds—arms joined and snaking down the streets twenty abreast—broke into the line of march, and Hylan gave up. From the rooftops and fire escapes of East Side tenements came the sounds of shofroth, blown by the rabbis of the Jewish immigrants who had settled there; everywhere "Over There" and "There's a Rose That Grows in No-Man's Land" were being sung.

It wasn't only the young girls who overwhelmed the military; crowds of all sorts of civilians surrounded soldiers and sailors and made them "prisoners of admiration." They were waltzed around willy-nilly, pounded on their backs, lifted onto shoulders and set down again, cheered and forced to make speeches only to have their words drowned out with applause. The Kaiser suddenly became a figure of fun. From the ravaging murderer of the world he had been only a few weeks before, Wilhelm Hohenzollern was now a joke. Mock groans and jeers went up whenever his name was mentioned. "Poor Bill! He tried to pinch off the world! He's gone!" one man cried.

What made the joke especially savory for the crowd, was not alone that the war was over and that the Kaiser had been beaten, but that he had run away—taking with him all his General Staff and his family and a trainful of food and wine. The Kaiser was burned in effigy as people cheered and waved their flags (somehow, nearly everyone seemed to have come into possession of a small American flag). On lower Fifth Avenue a group of men raised and lowered a dummy of the Kaiser from the top floor of an eight-story building with a rope not quite long enough to reach the heads of those on the sidewalk. As the figure came tumbling down, women passing below would scream and then break into laughter.

Since the celebration in New York centered mostly around mid-Manhattan, by early afternoon the midtown streets were all but impassable. Streetcars were stalled between crossings; drivers turned their motor- and horse-drawn trucks into public carriers, taking aboard everyone who could be jammed in. Airplane motors droned overhead, and subway caverns resonated with unusual noisiness. The din of horns, which swelled gradually hour after hour, had by afternoon grown into a continuous ear-shattering roar.

Fuel administrator Mercer P. Mosely announced at noon that the administration wanted New York City illuminated that night as never before. "Let us," said Mosely, "give the Kaiser a wake so bright and gorgeous that for the moment the memory of all the fires his armies started and all the guns his armies fired will be smothered and obscured."

"A great many statesmen made speeches during the day," observed the *Evening World,* "but nobody listened to them."

In London on that gray but pulsing day, the scene of rejoicing at the war's end was even more exalted than that in New York.

"It was a few minutes before the eleventh hour of the eleventh day of the eleventh month," wrote Winston Churchill in his sonorous prose.

> I stood at the window of my room looking up Northumberland Avenue towards Trafalgar Square, waiting for Big Ben to tell that the war was over. . . .
>
> And then suddenly the first stroke of the chime. I looked again at the broad street beneath me. It was deserted. From the portals of one of the large hotels . . . darted the slight figure of a girl clerk, distractedly gesticulating while another stroke of Big Ben resounded. Then from all sides men and women came scurrying into the street. Streams of people poured out of all the buildings. The bells of London began to clash. Northumberland Avenue was now crowded with people in hundreds, nay, thousands, rushing hither and thither in a frantic manner, shouting and screaming with joy. . . . Almost before the last stroke of the clock had died away, . . . London had become a triumphant pandemonium. . . .
>
> The ordeal was over. The peril had been warded off. The slaughter and the sacrifice . . . were at an end; and the over-strained people in the hour of deliverance gave themselves up for a space to the sensations of triumph. Church and state united in solemn thanskiving. The whole land made holiday. . . . All classes were mingled in universal rejoicing.

Nightfall brought no end to London's jubilation; an unceasing drizzle had no effect at all on a people who had lived through four years of death and fear and want. The lights were on again in Piccadilly Circus; all through the long hours crowds of people surged through the streets, oblivious of the rain and the cold. Headlines in the *Times* told the joyous story: REJOICINGS THROUGHOUT THE COUNTRY; KING'S MESSAGE TO THE EMPIRE—A PLEDGE REDEEMED, DANGER AND TRIUMPH SHARED; CROWDS AT ST. PAUL'S; REJOICING IN THE STREETS.

The most impressive thing about the service at St. Paul's Cathedral on that glorious day was the spontaneous, improvised, vibrant feel of it. The afternoon service was not normally heavily attended, but this day the nave was half full an hour before the service was due to start. When the service was begun, looking down from the choir stall above, nothing could be seen except humans, instead of the aisles and the pews themselves. Now there were crowds of people, many of whom had clearly come in on the spur of the moment. The service was spotted with the occasional cry of an infant and many of the worshipers were in clothes that showed that they had been on their way home from work when the appeal of the thanksgiving had overtaken them. There had, perhaps, been many more-splendid services at St. Paul's when the panoply of its ceremonies and the pomp of rank and power have been displayed. But it is doubtful that there had ever before been a service with such instinctive and profound expressions of deep and universal feeling.

One thing that struck many worshipers at the service was the number of people, particularly women, who wore black mourning clothes, for of the eight and a half million killed in the war, almost one million were British.

Across the channel from England, Ghent was a city to stage one of the most glorious of celebrations, for Ghent was the last Belgian city to be freed before the armistice. The Germans used Ghent as the hinge for their retreat to the northeast, and they held it with machine guns until the very last moment. Five hours after the Germans left, in the darkness of the early morning, a platoon of Belgian soldiers led by a young lieutenant moved in, and within minutes, as if by magic, it seemed that all the streets were filled with the citizens of Ghent shouting, cheering, embracing the soldiers and each other. Unlike New York or Washington, or even London or Paris, Ghent had known four long years of occupation and oppression, and its celebration was understandably gayer and more frenetic. To Ghent, November 11 was not only a day of armistice but the day of freedom. As dawn came, the bells of all the churches began to ring out, and all the ancient towers and belfries joined in sounding a cacophony of thanksgiving.

Soon the main division of the Belgian troops began to march in, and as the artillery went by, citizens covered the guns with flags, and the music of the bands was almost drowned out by the cheers of *Vive la Belgique*.

When darkness came to the ancient city of faded red brick Flemish houses with stepped gables, virtually unchanged since Charles II was in exile there, the tempo of the celebration seemed even more lively. For the first time since all the winters of the war the people could light their lamps and open their shutters, and from the windows streamed bright beams of light. Stars and a crescent moon turned the roofs of the buildings silver, cast patterns of lace in the squares beneath the trees, and laid shadowy blocks of white and black along the streets; and in this shimmering chiaroscuro the people of Ghent were out dancing and singing—dancing in groups with their arms linked; singing so that their voices, as a visitor wrote, "rose in a chorus from all over the city, like music by Debussy."

The following day, Ghent was still one vast cheering crowd as King Albert made his triumphal entry into the city. A brilliant sun now covered the old roofs of Ghent with a golden light, and the balconies of the buildings were emblazoned with banners and jammed with people. When the King and Queen and the young Prince rode by with an entourage of Belgian, French, and British generals, white flowers were thrown down to them from all the balconies, petals falling about like confetti. The royal party entered the reviewing stand outside the old club in the Place d'Armes, and a storm of cheers reverberated around them. Then the Belgian troops marched past, men who had fought on the Yser in the first days of the war, and men who, within the last few days, had fought their way toward Ghent with guns and cavalry. The King who had spent four years in the field with his men was now reviewing their victorious return. For the Belgians, the day was full.

Royalty was the focus of the celebrations in Britain and Belgium, and as the earth turned, in Paris it was the grand old man, now nearing eighty, Georges Clemenceau, "the Tiger," who drew the spotlight of the celebration. All of Paris—indeed, all of France—had known about the armistice since the early hours of the 11th, but it was not until well into the afternoon that Clemenceau entered the Chamber of Deputies and mounted into the tribune.

He waited for the applause to die down and without an introduction began to read the conditions of the armistice. (One was that the province of Alsace-Lorraine, lost in the war with Prussia nearly fifty years earlier, a war in which Clemenceau had voted not to surrender, would be returned to France.) The guns of victory began to boom along the Seine, but as the Premier read on, applause inside the chamber overwhelmed even the sound of the guns. When the speech was finished, the deputies rose applauding and cheering. Royalists on the right and Socialists on the left spontaneously broke into singing the "Marseillaise." The singing was taken up by the people in the galleries and spread to those jammed in the corridors outside, then to the people out in the streets and in the squares, to the vast crowds standing along the riverbanks. Parisians everywhere walked singing in the twilight.

As Belgium had suffered the occupation, so had northern France, and France also had the added bitterness—which was to color her attitude to the terms of the armistice and the peace, and to direct the course of her conduct for a decade and more—of the physical ravage of the war. The battlefield of Passchendaele was as desolate as the craters of the moon. Ypres, where tourists had trooped through the central square to admire the Cloth Hall surrounded by thousand-year-old houses, now was a vast ruin—shell-pocked roads twisting between mounds of rubble, grass and weeds overgrowing what had once been squares and highways. When the people who had lived there returned they could not tell where their homes had once stood or even where their streets had once been.

Now, as a poet put it, in this world the fires of hell had been put out. There was silence and the knowledge that now death was not perhaps the next artillery burst away. No more need the almost unbearable tenseness of waiting and listening and waiting more be endured. Now a sudden explosion did not paralyze the body with fear. (Most likely it was only an engineer detonating a land mine to make it harmless.) No longer did the evening mist silently spreading across the fields carry the possibility of poison gas; no more would there be the orders to move out at dawn.

At first in the stunning silence of the war's ending came the realization that you were still alive, that the gods had been either good or careless. Though others had died, you were alive. You had made it. It was a time when the small things of the earth filled the soul to overflowing. You listened to the rustle of the leaves and thought how lovely the sound is and how lucky you are to be enjoying it. These became the sounds of peace, the sounds you would hear henceforth; the eternal roar of the guns was a nightmare now over.

It was with sound—the blare of trumpets and the peal of organs—that the coming of peace was greeted at home. Where the fighting had been, for the first time in four years there was silence.

No sudden flares of gunlight, no sudden stabs of flame, no eerie glow above the shattered arms of trees, black against the near horizon.

Of course, the work of the armies was not finished, troops were still on the move, the Germans moving back, sullen, surly, the Allied troops moving ahead to the areas that they were to occupy, but now the columns moved openly in the daylight with their bands and their flags, and all along the lines there was laughing and singing and talking endlessly as though something had loosened every man's tongue and its sounds could not be stopped.

Staff cars streaked along the streets, dodging their way through the military traffic, and farm wagons were beginning to appear, and now and then, when night fell, rockets were fired from the staff cars and there would come gusts of laughter from young officers, shooting off their pistols into the darkness. Late at night, from the darkened villages of Belgium and northern France, there would suddenly blaze up into the black heavens the white streamers of flares that would reach the height of their trajectories, and burst in a great explosion of white light, then fall slowly back toward earth.

When the marching columns came through the villages, the soldiers shouted, *Guerre fini, guerre fini, Boche Kapoo!* and women and children came running to them with late-fall flowers, mostly red and white chrysanthemums, and stuck them on their tunics or in the straps of their steel helmets. Thousands of flags appeared suddenly in villages where no flag could have been shown without punishment until that very morning. Every gun team had a banner floating above the limber or the guns, and the horses had flowers in their harnesses. All the guns, even down to the rifles, had flowers protruding from their barrels, and the mud-gummed roads of war resembled a pageant, as seemingly endless tides of infantry, cavalry, artillery, and transport moved north and east, the banners of Belgium and France and England and America fluttering above them. Another tide moved the opposite way. Nowhere near as heroic a sight, though it too had flags and its banners, this pitiful band was made up of thousands of civilians, almost all men, who that morning had made their way back through the German lines. Taken from a thousand French and Belgian villages as conscript labor, now, at last, they were on their way home again.

A war as cruel and bitter as that of 1914–18, of course, could not end without some final evidence of individual cruelty and bitterness. On the last day, near a small village east of Valenciennes, a British battalion reached the edge of a wood and saw the small cluster of farm buildings that formed the village about five hundred yards away across the open fields. A patrol sent forward to scout the tiny village found a young German lieutenant, wounded, propped against a wall. The village was empty, he told them in English. The German rear guard had left two hours before. Accepting this at its face value (after all, the war was all but over, and the lieutenant did speak English), the British formed up and moved into the village square. While they were still in formation, German machine guns opened up from the roofs of buildings on all four sides of the square, and over a hundred of the British were killed before they were able to break ranks and start after the machine gunners. The machine gunners, even as they were being overrun, concentrated on finishing off the wounded lying in the square.

The British ended the fighting in a different way. At 10:50 A.M. on November 11, with only minutes to go, a squadron of His Majesty's 7th Dragoons was ordered forward to capture a bridge over the river Dendre at Lessines. (The official reason was that the bridge would be useful if the Germans later broke the terms of the armistice.) Along the straight road lined with trees, and in perfect formation, the squadron galloped forward—into the face of machine gun positions manned by the enemy. The Germans opened fire. The impetus of the charge carried some of the dragoons onto the bridge, but the position was not taken until several-score casualties had been suffered—and the machine gunners had ceased fire in accordance with the armistice instructions.

On the American front, the Germans apparently had large stocks of artillery ammunition which they had no desire to see unused, and throughout the whole of the morning they shelled the positions in front with a prodigality which was as haphazard as innate German efficiency would allow. Not unnaturally, the Americans replied. Moreover, as eleven o'clock drew nearer, the feeling apparently spread among the gun teams that as American artillery had not been present to fire the first shell of the war, it could at least make certain of firing the last.

This might not have mattered had it not been for the American propensity for competition. Each gun team wanted the doubtful honor for itself alone, and it is fatally easy, while ammunition lasts, to fire "just one more shot." The war therefore did not end at 11:00 A.M at all on the front between the Argonne and the Meuse, and it needed several orders from increasingly-high-ranking headquarters before the shelling finally ceased.

And with Gallic logic and reasonableness which compels admiration and strikes the happiest notes in the sorry tale of the morning's innumerable, wasteful tragedies, the French troops—once the news of the signing of the armistice reached them—did absolutely nothing but post sentries and stand ready to defend their positions against any suicidal attacks which the local German troops in the madness of despair might launch against them.

It is said that if one maintains a consistent attitude toward life's larger problems, circumstances will in the end conform to give the attitude validity: certainly on the morning of November 11 the French view of the value of French lives was justified.

By midday, silence here too lay across the battlefields like a blanket. Men climbed out of the rifle pits and trenches and stood erect in open country and felt a strange and uncomfortable sort of nakedness. Then, as the wonder and release from danger took hold of their minds, they became excited. They formed groups and stared at other groups forming that were not so far away in space, but until that moment had been divided from them by the psychology of war. Slowly, almost shyly, the groups approached each other. Often they would halt some few yards apart, while each member of each group scanned the faces of the men opposite, watching for the accustomed flash of ferocity. Then some movement or expression would break the tension and the groups would mingle, all shaking hands, all talking excitedly in an effort to break the incomprehension, exchanging souvenirs, the British and Americans forcing cigarettes on the Germans who had little to offer in exchange. Somehow wine appeared as it always does, and, of course, it was drunk.

By midafternoon the High Command was attempting to post pickets between the lines along almost the entire front, to prevent this fraternization. After all, if something happened to wreck the peace negotiations, then these men would have to go back to the trade of war: it would not do for them to become too friendly. But the High Command was whistling against the wind. The celebrations went on, and where the lines were close, shouted messages and singing hailed the end of the fighting, and when night fell, each side treated the other to fantastic firework displays of rockets, flares, signal lights, and explosives.

But neither jubilation nor goodwill between men of rival armies could cover the pock-marked face of war. Throughout much of Europe there were countless reminders of the war's fury. The battlefield of Flanders was but one example of the destructiveness that had been wrought—a destructiveness that outstripped the most bitter of human imaginings. The only road across the fields where poppies had grown was a four-mile stretch of rotting wooden planks winding along the crests of the ridges and occasionally collapsing into the acres upon acres of mud-and-water-filled shell holes. Almost no living thing was to be seen: just an occasional flurry of rats, and only rarely a bird, since there were no living plants to give sanctuary. Only an occasional rusting tank or a broken, overturned ammunition caisson relieved the bleak landscape of collapsed, gaping holes, which had been dugouts where men lived and died, of now-shattered concrete bunkers, of barbed wire in rusted tangles, of convex piles of corrugated iron. Faded crosses stood guard above innumerable graves which seemed to stretch toward infinity.

# II

## WAR'S DESOLATION

Warre brings spoile, and
spoile povertie, . . .
GEORGE PUTTENHAM

FOR THE FIRST TIME in modern warfare, the destruction of World War I extended far from the lines of combat. The damage would be greater in World War II, but war's new pattern emerged in the years 1914–18. When London was first hit from the air, there was the first faint precursor to the Battle of Britain, and to the ultimate bombing, Hiroshima. Along the great wide scar where the front had been, the destruction was so complete, the land so churned from shellfire and trenches, that it would take a generation to restore it. In the closing days of the war and in the frenzy of rage, the Germans covered miles of highways with magnificent trees that had once lined the sides of the roads; whole orchards were cut down, and fruit trees by the thousands lay in rows where they had been felled out of no motive save malice. Factories were blown up, their boilers exploded by bombs and their chimneys toppled as if the enemy were intent on destroying the whole world.

There could be joy in the West because of victory, but in the capitals to the east—in all the cities of the East, capitals to villages—it seemed as if Armageddon had indeed arrived. For one thing, no one had expected that World War I could last as long as it did. With the terrible new weapons of destruction, machine guns, gas, tanks, who could believe that even an animal as destructive as man could fight for four years? But, slowly, as the months passed, the elation of war oozed out and the grind of war set in. Even the triumphs that the newspapers continued to report were not enough to outbalance the endless, dreary days and weeks and months of fighting, of stalemate, of trench warfare, of bloodletting. Finally came the slow breakout from the trenches in 1918. The news of each battle was another blow to the peoples of the Central Powers: the Battle of the Somme just as spring began, the Battle of the Aisne, of Cantigny, Château-Thierry and Belleau Woods, and of the Meuse-Argonne, which lasted to the very day of the armistice. Even early in 1918, hope of victory still lingered in the hearts of the people in Germany, in Austria-Hungary, in Bulgaria and Turkey, because of the peace Vladimir Ilich Lenin had made with the Germans (after all, they had moved him secretly from Switzerland to Russia by way of Sweden to overthrow the government of Alexander Kerensky). Russia's capitulation meant that the Central Powers were no longer fighting a two-front war. But as the year wore on and the hot summer drifted toward the ice-cold mists of November, even hope had failed. The noose of defeat was tight about the neck of the Central Alliance. Bulgaria left the war on September 30 and Czar Ferdinand abdicated; the Turkish Armistice came a month later; the Austria-Hungarian Empire was cracking to the point that the Italians were able to defeat the Austrians at Vittorio Veneto.

To the very end, of course, there were German voices that demanded that the war go on. *Freundenblatt* (in Hamburg) warned that Germany must not permit herself to be "humiliated," and Berlin's *Tageblatt* argued that "so long as Germany's power has not collapsed" she need not abjectly submit to all Allied demands. But another Berlin paper, *Vorwarts* (printed on a single sheet of paper as were most of the east-of-the-Rhine papers that were still publishing in that dreadful autumn) counseled that Germany must accept any armistice terms because "while we indeed have the right to die ourselves, we have not the right to let others die."

In that autumn, horror was piled on horror, for three of the Four Horsemen of the Apocalypse—war, famine, and pestilence—were indeed abroad.

The influenza epidemic near the end of the war was so appalling that the medical world was "in an uproar," according to a University of Chicago bacteriologist, Edwin O. Jordan, who later wrote a book about it, *Epidemic Influenza.* The 1917–19 epidemic was given the name Spanish influenza because although outbreaks of influenza had been noticed on British army bases in France as early as the winter of 1916–17, the disease did not seem to reach formidable proportions until its outbreak in Spain in the spring of 1918.

The fatally insidious part of the epidemic was that not only did the medical profession lack a cure, but there was no way to halt its spread—and no other disease had ever spread so far so fast, according to the authorities of the day. Hardly had the first major outbreaks been noted in Spain than the disease was reported in army camps throughout France, England, and the United States, as well as in Russia, China, Japan, and India.

It was a killer disease, and it killed without discrimination: the white death rate was the equal of the Negro; male and female, rich and poor, all felt its ravages. Only age made a noticeable difference—the very young and the aged had the highest death rates. And no one knows how many deaths it was responsible for that were ascribed to similar ailments—pneumonia, whooping cough, tuberculosis, and that catchall of fatalities, heart disease. People walked down the streets of New York (and Boston and Philadelphia and San Francisco and Tokyo and Hong Kong) wearing masks constructed of antiseptic white cotton over their mouths and noses. A German article appearing in August of 1918 entitled "Die Spanische Krankheit ist Influenza vera" ("The Spanish Sickness Is True Influenza") points out:

> In 1918, as in previous epidemics, typical bewilderment was occurring as the result of the advent of a "new disease." [The "new disease" panic was occasioned by the astoundingly high death rate.] The meteorologists try to ascertain the course of the epidemic, the English recommend quinine as a panacea, and a new mistaken teaching in Germany seeks to explain the progress and intensity of the disease by malnutrition.

The war itself and the ending of the war somehow blurred the fact that the world was suffering the most calamitous epidemic in its history. Concurrent with the victory celebrations in London were scores of funerals, continuing past midnight, and the dirge of defeat in Berlin was deepened by lines of hearses bearing the victims of the disease to cemeteries. The epidemic far outstripped the war itself as a mass killer. The total slain in World War I is set at 8.5 million, but the number killed by influenza is put at 20 million. In India alone 12.5 million, or 4 percent of the total population, died in the epidemic. In the United States the disease took more than 500,000 lives.

It should not be surprising that German health authorities would ascribe the Spanish influenza deaths to malnutrition, for the military requirements in the closing months of the war and the rapacious vengeance of the Allies in the months after the armistice reduced the losers to a position of abjectness unparalleled in history except for the American Civil War. For much of Europe, peace brought the destruction of the entire economic system, as that of the Confederate States had been destroyed at the end of the Civil War.

Sir Norman Angell, who had argued in *The Grand Illusion,* published in 1910, that economic interests had become so powerful that war among the great powers was unthinkable, warned:

> By our political power we can create a Europe which, while not assuring advantage to the victor, deprives the vanquished of the means of existence. The loss of both ore and coal by the Central Powers might well make it impossible for their future populations to find food. What are they to do? Starve? To disclaim responsibility is to claim that we are entitled to use our power to deny them life.

It seemed, in short, that it is not that those who will not learn from history are compelled to repeat its mistakes; it is more, as Hegel commented, that "people and governments have never learned anything from history, or acted on principles deducible from it."

It is one thing to make the simple and obvious comment that the economic collapse of Europe after the war came out of the war's own almost incalculable destruction of what makes up an economy: natural resources and manpower. The war destroyed countless railways, factories, ships, and mines, and diverted twenty million men from productive to unproductive labor. Herbert Hoover pointed out: "The enemy collapsed not only from military and naval defeat but from total economic exhaustion." And

Hoover went on to add: "In this race to economic chaos, the European Allies were not far behind."

After the armistice an Allied blockade was imposed against Austria for four months, against Germany for eight months, against Russia for almost a year; and by a year after the armistice, the value of the German mark had fallen 80 percent, and the value of the Russian ruble was down 90 percent. Again it was Angell who—certainly as one of the first—emphasized one of the most obvious of the idiocies of the Allies:

> The famine has become so appalling that very great sums are collected in Britain and America for its relief. Yet the reduced productivity out of which the famine has arisen was quite obviously deliberately designed, and most elaborately planned by the economic provisions of the treaty and by the blockades prolonged after the armistice . . . and at the very time that advertisements were appearing in the *Daily Mail* for "Help to Starving Europe," and only a few weeks before France consented to advance money for the purpose of feeding Germany, that paper was working up "anti-Hun stunts" for the purpose of using our power to prevent any food at all from going to the Boches. It is also a duplication of the American phenomenon . . . : One bill before Congress for the loaning of American money to Europe in order that cotton and wheat may find a market: another bill before the same Congress designed, by a stiffly increased tariff, to keep out European goods so that the loans can never be repaid.

This was, indeed, what had become—and in World War II was even more to grow into—an extraordinary anomaly of modern warfare: at once a concept of total war and unconditional surrender, followed by binding up the wounds of the conquered. The concept of total war, in which the entire nation and not merely the military is involved, had been growing since Napoleonic days, an almost inevitable consequence of the Industrial Revolution. The destruction of a munitions factory or of a railroad marshaling yard, therefore, was as much a military victory as the capture of a town or the destruction of a division. This concept of total war came, too, at a time when the age of invention, most specifically the airplane, made it possible. The concepts both of unconditional surrender and of eventual reconstruction seem to have had their origin in the American Civil War. The fraternal bitterness of that holocaust led to a no-quarter-given-unless-the-white-flag-was-raised attitude. Nonetheless Abraham Lincoln and Andrew Johnson in sequitur determined that the southern states did not constitute a conquered nation, to be ruled as a capricious Congress saw fit, but had continuously remained a part of the Union and should be helped back to health, politically and economically, as rapidly as possible. The makers of the peace after World War I were not quite so magnanimous.

World War I also saw the beginning of propaganda as the world knows it today. Robert Hoe had invented the practical rotary press in 1846, but it was not until the end of the nineteenth century that newspaper publishers realized that with the Hoe press and the linotype machine, perfected by Ottmar Mergenthaler in the 1880's, the day of the mass-circulation newspaper had arrived. The new presses and other machines were far more expensive than the old equipment, but almost simultaneously the newspaper proprietors found it possible for them to turn a handsome profit on circulation (later supplemented by advertising and finally almost totally dependent on advertising). But to get mass circulation, the papers had to appeal to the basic (and often basest) emotions of the masses—curiosity, preoccupation with violence and sex, greed, and finally, but not least, patriotism. All through World War I the Allied press had carried on a Holy Crusade against the "Hun" and the "Boche." This campaign would reach such proportions at the coverage of the Versailles Peace Conference that the newspapers in general reported every move of the chief German delegate, Count Ulrich von Brockdorff-Rantzau, in such a way as to prove that he was at the very best an inhuman boor, if not a monster. Rantzau, for example, apparently because he was ill, delivered one statement while sitting down, but it prompted the British *Daily Mail* to comment that "after this, no one will treat the Huns as civilized or repentant." The *Mail* did not report what Rantzau had to say:

> I do not want to answer by reproaches to reproaches. . . . Crimes in war may not be excusable but they are committed in the struggle for victory and in the defense of national existence, and passions are aroused which make the conscience of peoples blunt. The hundreds of thousands of noncombatants who have perished since November 11 by reason of the blockade were killed with cold deliberation after our adversaries had conquered and victory had been assured them. Think of that when you speak of guilt and punishment.

Alfred F. Seligsberg, who wrote *Invalid Europe* (aimed at keeping the United States out of European affairs), commented too on the hatreds that had been exacerbated by the war. "The European continent today is a seething hell of hate," was his appraisal two years after the armistice.

> Life is oppressed by a pall of vindictiveness and mutual distrust. Wherever one goes, each country seems to hate some other country. The French hate the Germans and distrust the English. The Italians have all their old distrust and dislike of the Austrians, and hate the Jugoslavs, while they bitterly resent the lack of gratitude of the French, and feel that the Allies in general have ill-repaid their sacrifices.

France had been in the practice of hating (and distrusting) the Germans for a solid century, and France now regarded a defeated Germany much as a man who has beaten off a snake—no longer under attack, but not at all sure the enemy is dead. This ever-persistent attitude was to infect most of France's decisions until once again a French-German confrontation would lead to a world war.

And as for Italy at the end of the war, there was a good deal to be said for her attitude, and had her position at the Peace Conference been more fully understood, it might have spared Italy and the world some of the worst of the trials that were to come in the next twenty years. (Only *might,* of course; other factors were at work.) But Woodrow Wilson was preoccupied with his American Presbyterian idealism, and Lloyd George with the British elections. Clemenceau was understanding, but was old, and so Vittorio Orlando, without much won and without much firepower, was entitled to fume at the lack of consideration he received.

Even in the opening days of the war the Italian dedication to the dialectic of history and the eccentricity of her politics made her a doubtful asset as an ally. With Germany and Austria, for example, she was a member of the Triple Alliance, presumably balancing the so-called Triple Entente of Britain, France, and Russia, and yet hardly had the war started, than Italy announced that Germany had embarked on a war of aggression, rendering its pact void, and that Italy would remain neutral.

There was common sense behind this that the Italians could well have used later, and perhaps this could also partly explain Orlando's bitterness. Italy's way into the war was in a declaration of hostilities against Serbia, but there is no doubt that the motivation reached far back into the territorial imperative of irredentism. Even the word itself is an Italianate corruptive of "Italia irredenta," or "Italy unredeemed," and what Italy wanted to get out of the war were such pieces of real estate as Trieste, Istria, Fiume, and parts of Dalmatia—lands populated by an Italian majority, but held by Austria. Italy did get those lands eventually, but nonetheless the Italians felt that the Peace Conference itself was dominated on all substantive issues by Clemenceau and Lloyd George, and on propaganda issues by Wilson.

Most Europeans days then, beyond the peace conference and the Spanish influenza, were dominated by efforts to overcome the chaos that war had brought to the land. In most of the countries between the Rhine and the Urals, leather, wool, and cotton had virtually disappeared. Shirts and skirts were made of paper, and shoes had wooden soles. All foods, of course, were rationed, as they were in France and England (and to a very minor extent in the United States), but in the Central European countries the rationing was severe indeed. In Germany poor quality meat was limited to 4.75 ounces per person per week, about an eighth of prewar consumption. (Rationing was essentially confined to the cities and the towns; in time of war the peasant farmer always fares better than the city folk.)

Before the war Germany had annually imported about 40 percent of her consumption of eggs—170,000 tons. By 1917 the figure had fallen to less than 10 percent, and in the ten months of 1918 before the armistice, to only 4 percent. Similarly, whereas before the war the importation of fish had been half of the consumption, it had dropped in the ten months of 1918 to less than a seventh. Milk, too, was in short supply and butter was almost nonexistent; of necessity the peoples of Central Europe had virtually become vegetarians. A survey of all German cities and towns with over five thousand population showed an average weight loss of 20 percent, with the medical consequences of reduced mental and physical capacities. Diseases normally under control had reappeared; the birthrate was down; doctors reported retarded recovery from all diseases and a marked increase in mortality and morbidity, especially among old people and children.

For example, mortality figures for the German civilian population showed no percentage increase for 1914 over 1913, but during the war years a sharp increase in the rate occurred. From 1913 to 1918 the death rate of women in childbirth rose 14 percent; tuberculosis deaths 100 percent; and in the five-to-fifteen age group 55 percent.

In his *American Epic* Herbert Hoover notes:

> There is a decreased resistance to disease in all cases of marked starvation. . . . the prolonged starvation by millions of people in Europe during the present war is demonstrating anew the fact that the individual, weakened by lack of food, falls an easier prey to all infectious diseases, and we have thus in a starving society an increased incidence of infectious diseases and an increased death rate, quite apart from deaths due to actual starvation. . . . There is nearly always an increase of gastro-enteric diseases—diarrhoea, dysentery, etc.—in a starving society, because starving peoples are forced to consume spoiled or unsuitable foods and food substitutes. . . .

Starving children are especially susceptible to a faulty growth of the bones, rickets, and relief investigators found that rickets had now reached epidemic proportions, though the disease had been almost unknown in peacetime. In addition, among starving adults, months of underfeeding had induced a type of dropsy—called War edema or Hunger edema, an almost certain prelude to death. A further problem was tuberculosis. The cure of tuberculosis in those days was an extremely uncertain and always long-drawn-out process, and even to begin to effect a cure required, among other things, a wholesome diet that was not easily provided even in the countries that had won the war much less in those that had lost. Tuberculosis was soon spreading by geometric progression. Each new case served to infect more starvation-weakened people until, as one heartsick investigator reported, it seemed that all of Eastern Europe was a giant tuberculosis sanitorium. As Hoover pointed out, the physical and mental weaklings produced by starvation were likely to beget their kind, to the detriment of future generations. "The starved, the subnormal, the dwarfed, and the tubercular child can perchance be reclaimed, cured, and rendered useful members of society," wrote Hoover. "If this is not done, the injury to the race . . . will in many countries be more severe than that due to the loss of vigorous manhood on the field of battle." The American Relief Administration, which Hoover headed, found that conditions varied widely: in some regions 90 percent of the children under ten years of age were seriously starved, and 10–25 percent stunted; 30–60 percent of the adult population had lost an average of 30–35 percent of normal body weight." The one note of optimism was in the great recuperative powers of young people, which, it was hoped, would allow a large majority of the starved and stunted children to be "salvaged," even though they had been on subnormal diets for a long period of time.

The American Relief Administration helped a total of six and a half million persons, virtually all of them children or expectant mothers. This did not include the millions assisted by such other big charitable agencies as the American Red Cross, the Jewish Joint Distribution Committee, the Near East Relief Committee, and the American Friends Service Committee, who also joined in combating famine.

Even when starvation was absent, diets of root stocks, herbs, and bulbs were commonplace. Autopsies on persons who died of starvation often revealed wood and sand in the stomach, eaten to ease the ache of endless hunger. One of the major reasons for the massive starvation was the loss of European livestock—especially heavy in the Central European countries where starvation was most severe. The number of cattle herds had dropped from 98.3 million prewar to 79.9 million; hogs from 69.3 million to 29.6 million and sheep from 190.8 million to 104.8 million.

As a result of the diminishing stock of animals, Hoover felt that animal products would necessarily continue to be imported, "provided the resources can be found to pay for them."

Germany was especially hard hit because during the period of the armistice official American relief was cut off by the so-called Lodge Amendment. This piece of legislation, sponsored by Henry Cabot Lodge, forbade the use of any Congressional appropriations for relief in enemy countries. And even after the peace conference the outlook for the nation remained about as bleak, since a good part of her eastern "breadbasket" had been ceded to Poland, cutting German grain and sugar beet production by about a third. Hoover himself was troubled by the American behavior: "Great as were the German outrages [of the war], there was scarcely an American at the peace conference who believed that the signed papers would hold the sick giant that was the German race. And we were in despair over the dragon's teeth from which would grow the evil jinn of the future."

The dilemma that Germany faced was summarized in the report made to the peace conference by the German Economic Commission:

> After the diminution of [Germany's] products, after the economic depression from the loss of her colonies, her merchant fleet, and her foreign investments, Germany will not be in a position to import from abroad an adequate quantity of raw material. An enormous part of German industry

will, therefore, be condemned inevitably to destruction. The need of importing foodstuffs will increase considerably at the same time that the possibility of satisfying this demand is as greatly diminished. In a very short time, therefore, Germany will not be in a position to give bread and work to her numerous millions of inhabitants, who are prevented from earning their livelihood by navigation and trade. These persons should emigrate, but this is a material impossibility, all the more because many countries and the most important ones will oppose any German immigration. To put the peace conditions into execution woul logically involve, therefore, the loss of several millions of persons in Germany. This catastrophe would not be long in coming about, seeing that the health of the population has been broken down during the war by the blockade, and during the armistice by the aggravation of the blockade by famine. No help, however great, or over however long a period it were continued, could prevent these deaths *en masse*.

We do not know, and indeed we doubt, whether the Allies and Associated Powers realize the inevitable consequences which will take place if Germany, an industrial state, very thickly populated, closely bound up with the economic system of the world, and under the necessity of importing enormous quantities of raw material and foodstuffs, suddenly finds herself pushed back to the phase of her development, which corresponds to her economic status and the numbers of her population as they were half a century ago. Those who sign this treaty will sign the death sentence of many millions of German men, women, and children.

The necessity of endlessly cataloguing the miseries of people long dead and long forgotten is painful. Forgetfulness, as has been observed, makes living possible. But to understand what would happen in the next two decades, when most of Europe would come under the control of dictators, it must be remembered that the road for those dictators was cleared largely by what the people of those countries went through in the terrible winter after the war.

The Chief Commissioner of Livestock for Scotland, appointed by the British Government to investigate food conditions in Germany, described the "rotten and putrid" potatoes which he saw being prepared for sale in the poorer districts of Berlin: "No farmer in Britain would dream of attempting to give this load of potatoes to any animal on his farm. . . . It was with difficulty that one could believe these potatoes . . . could be eaten by any human creatures; only the pangs of direct hunger would make their consumption possible."

A British doctor in Hungary told of hospital blankets so worn out that they could no longer be disinfected, of newborn children wrapped in rags—and sent home at the end of ten days, with their mothers—alike fated to die of cold and hunger. Bandages in the Balassa Hospital were made from paper, the doctor reported. "The swaddling clothes for infants," he explained, "are half paper, half cotton, and are bad for the babies' skins, and useless after three washings."

The report chief of the British mission to prisoners of war in Austria-Hungary stated:

> It is my deliberate opinion as a doctor that unless food is sent to Vienna immediately, at least 200,000 people out of a total population of 2,500,000 will die as soon as the cold weather sets in. Vienna is not on the verge of starvation, but actually starving, and people are dying like flies. During the whole of my fifteen years' medical experience in India, I have never witnessed such sights as these in Vienna. Food had begun to be sent in by the Allies; but not enough, and since the blockade was still maintained, and as Austria could purchase neither food nor raw materials for herself, the state of the population became terrible. Cabbages and turnips became the main staples. The milk ration, even for infants, was about a teacupful. The mortality was appalling, and there was no wood left for coffins. Boxes served as coffins for the children (thirty or forty were dying per day in one institution); but grown-up bodies had to be buried in mass graves, the bodies one over the other, with a layer of earth and lime in between. Under blockade conditions, too, no linen could

> be spared for graveclothes. The dead were wrapped in paper and carried out of town by night. During these months [November of 1918 to March of 1919], there were ample stocks of necessaries near at hand. In Switzerland, large stocks of substitute flour, which could no longer find sale in Switzerland, were threatening to go bad. Warehouses were congested with cotton goods, which Switzerland was not allowed to offer for sale. But the blockade was strictly enforced by the Inter-Allied Commission, without whose permission nothing could be exported from Switzerland.

It was estimated that 96 percent of the children in Vienna—340,000—were undernourished, and the American Relief Association could feed only 8,000 a day; thus admission to the soup kitchen was given only to those on the verge of starvation.

Even Vienna's jails, including the central jail, as described by a visitor, had their own horror story.

> Only one out of every four prisoners have beds, and personal linen is changed only once a month; the overcrowded, verminous cells are jammed with prisoners, the majority of whom have not yet been brought to trial; frequent riots are quelled by flooding the cells to the depth of a yard; many children are in jail—starvation had caused tendency to theft; children fourteen and up were kept in adult cells; there was one ward full of pregnant women accused of theft—pregnant women were one of the few groups segregated; there were many ex-soldiers; one with medals tatooed on his chest—Iron Cross and, below it, in a line, all the service medals, starting with the 1914.

Other more vengeful human feelings began to manifest themselves now that the war was over; the general attitude of the peace conference was to extract every ounce of economic vengeance it could, and this was to exacerbate the situation beyond measure.

It is difficult to dream of, and as hard to describe, the terrible days that the Russian people experienced in the course of war followed by revolution. At the mercy of the warring armies and the rapacious bands of raiding gangs, they were also going through one of the most terrible famines in history—one that helps make Herbert Hoover's *American Epic* such grim reading. Hoover estimates that about 25 million people were faced with absolute famine in an area that covered 750,000 square miles in the Volga River Valley and about 85,000 square miles in the Ukraine. Typhus, cholera, typhoid, smallpox, and fever swept the area; millions of panic-stricken people attempted to flee on foot, by rail, by any sort of conveyance, moving into other parts of Russia already short of food, carrying infection with them.

All the cities of Russia were filled with these refugees, camping on the floors of the railroad stations and on the streets around, vast camps of the destitute with their pitiful handloads of belongings, all waiting to go somewhere else, wherever it was, because there was nothing here, forcing their way into freight cars and simply staying there, waiting for it to leave, whenever and wherever it was going. When trains came in they would rush to them by the hundreds; a few successful ones would ride off, the rest would return to wait. Whatever the weather, the trains were jammed, coaches, boxcars, and flatcars alike; refugees crowded the ledges between cars and stood upon the couplings. There was no system; it was a mystery to observers that as many seemed to be traveling from east to west as from west to east. Relief workers, on the border of Latvia, met a fifty-eight-boxcar train jammed with refugees that had been traveling for twenty-one days.

A relief report from Orenburg, where the country was covered with six feet of snow, said:

> Conditions in Orenburg City itself are almost beyond description. Poverty, malnutrition, and starvation are evident everywhere: the dead seen lying on the streets of the city and on the roads leading into town soon become prey to dogs and birds. The sick and the starving are collected into public homes without facilities to care for them. "Dom Ivanoff," a collecting station for adults and children, is one of the worst of these institutions. Its capacity is three thousand, but capacity now means the number of persons that can be packed on all the floors of the building, leaving here and there a narrow

> aisle to allow ingress and egress to carry out the dead. Starving, sick, and dying are crowded together upon the floors, fifty to one hundred in a room. There are no toilet facilities and no bathing accommodations except a cold spigot in the court. The government ration consists of a quarter pound of bread and some hot water daily. The dead—we saw as many as three in a single room lying among the living—are carried out and piled naked together to be transported later to the cemetery where great pits, approximately ten feet deep and accommodating several hundreds of bodies, are dug. These receive all the city dead, about eight hundred a day.

The Orenburg district relief office was opened November 9, when the death rate from starvation was four hundred per day and on the increase. The railroad station was jammed with filthy refugees of all ages, starving and with no hopes of obtaining food. As at all other stations they seemed to be waiting for trains for anywhere and when they got there they boarded another train for somewhere else. The dead lay in the streets for days on end. In the pest holes termed "Children's Homes" as many as one thousand children would be housed in space for four hundred with no food, no fuel, from forty to fifty dying a day. Horses and camels dropped in the streets and could not get up. The relief report continued:

> General conditions in the premises: no mattresses, beds, blankets, or clothing. Lying on bare floors huddled together in an effort to keep warm. Inmates alive with vermin; wearing such clothes as they had when they came in. Such a demoralizing, depressing, and sickening sight has never before been seen by Americans. Cannibalism reported and authenticated. Bodies too numerous to bury and which had died of typhus and other diseases and were piled in heaps in buildings, were stolen, and the flesh boiled for food. The punishment meted to offenders was to imprison them until they died of starvation, with the exception of minors who were accessories to the cases, who were released after the older persons concerned with them were dead. A strong guard had to

> be maintained over the American Relief Agency warehouse during the entire winter. The building was attacked several times by persons who attempted to get past the guards; the latter were forced to fire and several were killed at the gates as they tried to force their way in. Lawlessness, robberies, and murders are extremely common and it is not safe to venture out upon the streets at night in Orenburg. Those who must be out keep to the center of the streets and avoid passing near vacant buildings as the Khargises, adept with the lasso, are reported using them to haul people up from the sidewalks, for the purpose of robbery and murder.

It was small wonder that of these days, Trotsky wrote: "One unconsciously asked the question whether the life forces of the exhausted, shattered, despairing land would last until the new regime was in the saddle. Provisions were not at hand. There was no army. The state apparatus was being put together. Conspiracies were festering everywhere. The Czechoslovak army stood on our soil as an independent power. We could offer almost no opposition to them."

Perhaps the postwar economic situation could have been redeemed, but now war and peace had combined to destroy so many European prewar institutions that had existed for a hundred years that a whole Europe would have to be built. On the other hand, A. J. P. Taylor, in *The First World War,* agreeing that the industrial plant of Europe had been damaged—but not enough to wreck the continent—argued:

> On a map of Europe, the areas of destruction appear as tiny black spots: northeastern France, parts of Poland and Serbia, a remote corner of Italy. Against this, though less noticed, were the new industrial resources which the war had called into existence. All the destruction was put right within a few years, so that it was soon hard to find the evidence that there had been a great war. Most countries surpassed their prewar production by 1925. Even Soviet Russia reached the level of 1913 again by 1927. At the end of the war, men like J. M.

> Keynes thought that the great problem of the future would be general poverty: they imagined that productive powers had been permanently reduced. Instead, within ten years, overproduction became the great problem of mankind. The war, far from weakening economic resources, stimulated them too much. The most serious blow inflicted by the war economically was to men's minds, not to their productive powers. The old order of financial stability was shaken, never to be restored. Depreciated currencies, reparations, war debts, were the great shadows of the interwar period—all imaginary things, divorced from the realities of mine and factory.

It was the "imaginary things" that in the end were to turn out to be the important ones. The easiest thing for man to replenish is manpower, and this was done first. A prolific mammal, with increasingly near-total control of his environment, neither war nor famine has been able to control man's growth; the total population of the world in 1920 was 15 percent greater than it was in 1914. But depreciated currencies, reparations, war debts, assumed their own reality, and their shadow foretold the events that would again devastate the continent. Looking back now, it is clear that none of the leaders of the western world realized how completely the fabric of the world had been sundered. Winston Churchill wrote of the departures of the captains and the kings in majestic tones, like the chroniclers of the wars of the monarchies through ages past. But formerly, crowned heads had fought their generation's war, won or lost, then prepared for the war still to be fought by their successors. But no one—Churchill, Lloyd George, Clemenceau, Marshal Ferdinand Foch, Orlando, Colonel Edward M. House, or Wilson—seemed to grasp that the tornado of war had sucked out a vacuum in Central Europe, that the old order had vanished not metaphorically but literally.

In the hospital at Pasewalk in Pomerania, Bavaria, where the "piercing pain in the eye sockets" that he had suffered since the gas attack on the front near Werwick on October 13 was now abating, Adolf Hitler had his own version of what had happened. And his own psychotic, Jew-haunted being, in a little over a quarter of a century, was to provide the form, the meaning, and the authority lacking in Central Europe after the war. The day of the emperor had vanished and the day of the dictator would arrive. The western democracies—a bit outmoded and old-fashioned, a bit seedy and down at the heels, and for the moment, politically incompetent and economically impotent—stood on the outside of this new age, looking in.

# MAKING PEACE

The most disadvantageous
peace is better than
the most just war.

ERASMUS

ON JANUARY 8, 1918, WOODROW WILSON made the famous speech that outlined, in idealistic and vague terms, the war aims of the Allies. These aims were reduced to "fourteen points": (1) open covenants among nations and the termination of secret diplomacy, (2) freedom of navigation of the high seas in peace and war, (3) removal of economic barriers to trade among nations, (4) reduction of national armaments, (5) adjustment of all colonial claims impartially in the interest of both the subject peoples and the nations involved, (6) evacuation of Russia, (7) evacuation of Belgium, (8) evacuation of French territory and adjustment of the Alsace-Lorraine issue, (9) readjustment of Italy's frontiers along clearly recognizable lines of nationality, (10) autonomous development to be accorded the people of Austria-Hungary, (11) evacuation of Serbia, Montenegro, and Rumania (the Balkan States) with access to the sea for Serbia, (12) sovereignty to be secured to the Turkish minorities of the Ottoman Empire and autonomy for other portions of the Empire, (13) an independent Poland to be established that would include all territories inhabited by Polish people, (14) creation of "a general association of nations" to provide "mutual guarantees of political independence and territorial integrity to great and small states alike."

The Fourteen Points were widely acclaimed not alone by the Allied nations but among subjected minorities within the Austrian and Ottoman Empires. In the German Empire they were seen as a promise of leniency if the country became a democracy. When in the summer of 1918 the German commanders realized the inevitability of defeat, the new Chancellor, Prince Max of Baden, let it be known that the Fourteen Points were acceptable to him as conditions for discussion of an armistice.

Yet, in November, Woodrow Wilson would address a Republican-dominated Congress which was, perhaps, the least responsive and the least effective that any president ever confronted. (Americans of the day were amused by a vaudeville routine that suggested: "If you're not smart enough to teach, and too stupid to steal and you still don't want to work—run for Congress!") Wilson, as an Ivy League intellectual, never seemed able to comprehend the parochial mind of the average Congressman. America then was still basically rural or semirural, so that the average member of the House of Representatives came from either a farming district or a very small town where the big event of the day was the arrival of the milk train; or if he came from a city it was likely to be one of the grimy, heavy-industry slum breeders on the Ohio or the Allegheny, or one of the immigrant-crowded seaports in the Northeast. In any event, the average Congressman was very unlikely to be interested in either Wilson's high-flown dedication to idealism or the morality of his plans for a new Europe. It has been said that "the average American felt . . . that while his government could perhaps not have avoided the war, the war ought somehow to have avoided America; that it was unpleasant for a quiet gentleman who happened to be a spectator of a street fight suddenly to be forced to use his fists to protect his own head."

Against such a background Wilson delivered his address to Congress on November 11. After the formal opening, listing the terms of the armistice, Wilson continued with his message to the world:

> We know too that the object of war is attained; the object upon which all free men had set their hearts; and attained with a sweeping completeness which even now we do not realize. Armed imperialism, such as the men conceived who were but yesterday the masters of Germany, is at an end, its illicit ambitions engulfed in black disaster. Who will now seek to revive it?
>
> The great nations . . . have now definitely united in the common purpose . . . to set up such a peace as will satisfy the longing of the whole world for disinterested justice, embodied in settlements which are based upon something much better and much more lasting than the selfish competitive

> interests of powerful states. There is no longer conjecture as to the objects the victors have in mind. They have a mind in the matter, not only, but a heart also. Their avowed and concerted purpose is to satisfy and protect the weak as well as to accord their just rights to the strong.

From the bloody writhing of revolution then springing up in Europe, especially in Russia, Wilson drew an extraordinarily optimistic conclusion:

> Disorder immediately defeats itself. If excesses should occur, if disorder should for a time raise its head, a sober second thought will come and a day of constructive action, if we help and do not hinder. . . .
>
> The present and all that it holds belong to the nations and the peoples who preserve their self-control and the orderly processes of their goverments; the future to those who prove themselves the true friends of mankind. To conquer with arms is to make only a temporary conquest; to conquer the world by earning its esteem is to make permanent conquest. I am confident that the nations that have learned the discipline of freedom and that have settled with self-possession to its ordered practice are now about to make conquest of the world by the sheer power of example and of friendly helpfulness.

As Wilson delivered his address, given a better comprehension of the mood of Congress, he might have seen before him in the Capitol chamber the signals of the coming defeat of the world peace project closest to his heart. An eyewitness reported that barely half the membership of Congress was present (in part because the elections had been held barely a week before, and some members of Congress were not back in Washington; in November of 1918 civilian air traffic in the United States was still nonexistent). Applause was sparse. When the President announced that the fighting had stopped, there was a round of polite handclapping such as might have greeted the announcement that a statue by a renowned American sculptress had had the honor to be accepted by the French Government for exhibition in the Luxembourg Gardens (which had happened that year to Malvina Hoffman's "Bacchanale").

The only sustained applause, the only real cheering, came when Wilson announced that German troops had already begun the evacuation of France, Belgium, Luxembourg, and more significantly of Alsace-Lorraine. Faint applause followed the announcement that the Supreme War Council had agreed to send food to the famishing peoples of the Central Powers; nor did enthusiasm increase at the conclusion of the speech, which was devoted to an appeal for mercy to the German people. "The suggestion of a charitable and helpful attitude toward Germany, however," reported *Current History,* "brought no demonstrations from those who listened to the President."

At least part of the credit—or blame—for Wilson's approach to the occasion goes to Colonel House, a determinedly self-effacing small Texan (about five feet seven) who had first met Wilson at the 1912 Democratic National Convention that had nominated Wilson for President. House had a burning need to be close to the seats of power, and enough money to indulge it. As adviser to a series of Texas governors, he had been given the honorary title of Colonel. House had long since been sent to Paris by Wilson as more or less his personal representative; House had cabled the President on November 10:

> Would suggest that when the armistic is signed that you read the terms to Congress and use the occasion to give another message to the world. You have a right to assume that the two great features of the armistice are the defeat of German military imperialism and the acceptance by the Allied Powers of the kind of peace the world has longed for. A steadying note seems to me necessary at this time. A word of warning and a word of hope should be said. The world is in ferment and civilization itself is wavering in the balance.

At the announcement of the armistice in Paris, House cabled: "Autocracy is dead. Long live democracy and its immortal leader. In this great hour my heart goes out to you in pride, admiration, and love."

Jan Christiaan Smuts, later to be the long-term Prime Minister of South Africa, and evidently more perceptive than Wilson, took a different view of postwar developments:

> There is a serious danger that the bad, but more or less orderly, political prewar system of Europe may give place to a wild disorder of jarring and warring state fragments, such as we now see on a vast scale in Russia. . . . What is going to happen when, as now seems probable, Austria breaks up and becomes a "Balkans" on a vaster scale? With the creation of an "independent" Poland, there will be a chain of these discordant fragments right across Europe from Finland in the north to Turkey in the south. No League of Nations could hope to prevent a wild war dance of these so-called free nations in the future.

Wilson, for all his insistence on the self-determination of small nations, had not really given enough thought to what a nation was, nor whether it ought to be independent, or even what independence means. What is a nation, for example? "The miracle of political independence," said Benjamin Disraeli. "A portion of mankind united among themselves by common sympathies which do not exist between them and any others," said John Stuart Mill. "A group of men who speak one language and read the same newspapers," said Nietzsche. Shakespeare put it most poetically, of course: "This royal throne of kings, this scepter'd isle, this earth of majesty, this seat of Mars, this other Eden, demi-paradise, this fortress built by nature for herself against infection and the hand of war, this happy breed of men, this little world, this precious stone set in the silver sea, which serves it in the office of a wall or as a moat defensive to the house, against the envy of less happier lands, this blessed plot, this earth, this realm, this England. . . ." Not to overlook the United States Declaration of Independence which asserted that "as Free and Independent States, they have full power to levy War, conclude Peace, contract Alliances, establish Commerce, and to do all other Acts and Things which Independent States may of right do."

Others would also be skeptical of Wilson's vision for a world at peace. Gustav Stresemann, later to be Chancellor and Foreign

Minister of Germany, was frankly suspicious. In late October he wrote:

> I have the greatest mistrust of Wilson, and I believe he will lure us from concession to concession until we surrender unconditionally and are utterly helpless like a piece of cloth under the tailor's scissors. As far as I can see, Wilson's Fourteen Points already present the possibility of the loss of Alsace-Lorraine, Upper Silesia, Posen, and parts of West Prussia, and in addition an undefined sum for damages, which could very easily be transformed into a war indemnity, however otherwise it may be disguised. The loss of the iron works in Alsace-Lorraine and the coal mines in Upper Silesia would strike at the very vitals of our economic existence. And if in addition we are to make ourselves liable for a war indemnity running into tens of milliards, we shall be paralyzed for a century.

Stresemann's logic, though unassailable, could hardly have been persuasive to his enemies, since by now Germany's defeat could be foreseen.

At his home at Oyster Bay, Long Island, Theodore Roosevelt, the nation's twenty-sixth President, was flat on his back with the gout but wrote his son Theodore, Jr.:

> We have lived through the most tremendous tragedy in the history of civilization. We should be sternly thankful that the tragedy ended with a grim appropriateness, too often lacking. All the people directly or indirectly responsible for the tragedy, all those who have preached and practiced the cynical treachery, brutality and barbarism and the conscienceless worshiping of revolting cunning and brute force which made the German people what it was in 1914 (and what, except that it is defeated, it now is)—all these people have come down in the crash. When the war first broke out I did not think the Kaiser was really to blame. I thought he was simply the tool; gradually I was forced to realize that he was one of the leading conspirators, plotters, and wrongdoers. The

> last fortnight has shown that he was not even a valorous barbarian. . . . Think of the Kaiser and his six sons saving their own worthless carcasses at the end, leaving their women, like their honor, behind them.

Roosevelt's ire was not directed against only the Kaiser and the German people; Woodrow Wilson and the Fourteen Points were as scathingly denounced. In Roosevelt's eyes Wilson intended—through a negotiated peace—to "double-cross" the Allies, while posing as the "umpire" between the Allied and Central powers, thereby enlarging his own personal popularity and gaining political advantage for his party. Calling himself the "chief factor" in thwarting Wilson's aims and crediting himself with having thus "rendered substantial service to the Allies," Roosevelt explained to his son that *"the Fourteen Points were thoroughly mischievous"* because they *"would have meant a negotiated peace with Germany"* (Italics added).

If Roosevelt's views had merely been those of a former President, it would have been bad enough, but he was possibly one of the best-known Americans in the world. At almost the same time Colonel House was threatening that America would pursue a separate peace unless Wilson's Fourteen Points were used as the basis for negotiating an armistice, Roosevelt's attitude was a considerable factor leading to the opposition's adoption of the "hard line."

House confided to his diary how that opposition was countered. He had awakened at three o'clock in the morning, and:

> I fell to thinking about the dilemma I was in with the three Prime Ministers. It then occurred to me there was a way out of the difficulty. I would tell them that if they did not accept the President's Fourteen Points and other terms enunciated since January 8, I would advise the President to go before Congress and lay the facts before it, giving the terms which England, France, and Italy insisted upon, and ask the advice of Congress whether the United States should make peace with Germany now that she has accepted the American terms, or whether we should go on fighting until

> Germany had accepted the terms of France, England, and Italy, whatever they might be. . . . I turned over and went to sleep, knowing I had found the solution of a very troublesome problem.

Young Walter Lippmann, working with Frank Cobb, editor of the New York *World,* and Colonel House, wrote to House when the Allies concurred on the Fourteen Points: "Frankly I did not believe it was humanly feasible, under conditions as they seemed to be in Europe, to win so glorious a victory."

Even as Winston Churchill looked down from his office window upon Londoners celebrating the armistice, he was thinking beyond the rites of rejoicing. The problems of peace loomed now and would have to be faced up to. He was already grappling with the question of how to employ three million munitions workers no longer needed, and how well demobilization, long ago planned, would work. And he was worried whether Woodrow Wilson was astute enough to realize the depth of significance of the election returns of November 5, 1918. The United States Senate barely went Republican, but Republican it went, and so Wilson's most bitter opponent, Henry Cabot Lodge, would be a figure of great importance in the crucial years ahead. By thirty-seven seats the House of Representatives also went Republican (Calvin Coolidge was elected Governor of Massachusetts; Henry Ford was defeated for Senator from Michigan by Truman H. Newberry).

Churchill wrote of his dream of the three great men of the world coming to grips with the new reality: of Wilson, who realized that he must try to drum up Republican support for the peace treaty that the Senate would eventually have to ratify and for his dream that the United States join the anticipated League of Nations. Churchill also dreamed of a Georges Clemenceau able to master his overweening fear-hatred of the Germans; of a Lloyd George able to put aside his personal political ambitions in the hope that history would be kind to him if he did not "fall below the level of events upon the greatest occasions."

Not that Lloyd George himself was insensible to the occasion. "No settlement which contravenes the principles of eternal justice will be a permanent one," he said the day after the armistice. "Let us be warned by the example of 1871. We must not allow any sense of revenge, any spirit of greed, any grasping desire, to override the fundamental spirit of righteousness. Vigorous attempts will be made to hector and bully the government in the endeavor to make them depart from the strict principles of right and to satisfy some base, sordid, squalid ideas of vengeance and of avarice."

H. G. Wells, one of the great phrasemakers of his age ("the war to end war") also hoped that in the hour of victory Britain would "save the liberated Germans from vindictive treatment." The war of the giants has ended, Churchill commented; the quarrels of pygmies have begun.

On December 4, 1918, Woodrow Wilson and his party of advisers sailed aboard the *George Washington* for the Paris talks. His reception by the people in Europe must have been one of the President's great moments of personal acclaim. Since he had reached Europe a few days before the conference would convene, Wilson made trips to England and Italy, and everywhere throngs gathered to cheer him.

On January 12, 1919, the first formal session got under way in a plenary session that because of its attendant confusion was described by one writer as suggesting "that sense of riot in a parrot house." To achieve less unwieldy meetings smaller sessions were soon instituted: at first a Council of Ten and later a Council of Four—the so-called Big Four. The members, besides President Wilson, were David Lloyd George, Prime Minister of Great Britain, Georges Clemenceau, President of the Council of France, and Vittorio Orlando, Premier of Italy. Because Orlando would frequently absent himself from the deliberations, many of the decisions affecting the destiny of the world were made by "three lone men in a room." No matter what their final place in history, at that moment they looked like titans.

Considering the similarities between the terms of the Versailles Treaty and those of the Treaty of Brest-Litovsk, it is anomalous that the latter be so little heard of. Despite the incredible success of the Bolshevik Revolution in November of 1917—or perhaps because of it—the new government of Russia, racked by civil war and ravaged by famine, had to accept the terms that the Germans wanted to impose. And, as the Allies were to do to Germany later, the German Government, driven by the twin motives of greed and fear (the ever-present fear of the Russian bear), imposed extremely harsh terms. As a result of the treaty, Russia lost 34 percent of her population, 32 percent of her agricultural lands, 85 percent of her beet-sugar land, 54 percent of her industrial undertakings, and 89 percent of her coal mines. Compared to this, the Treaty of Versailles seems almost generous, and may help explain the special brutality of the war that was to come a generation later.

The German High Command tried to justify the severity of the terms from the standpoint of military considerations, but ironically the very harshness of the peace meant that its terms could be maintained only by overwhelming force. This compelled General Erich Ludendorff to keep more than a million soldiers in the east at a time when every bit of available manpower was needed for the fighting in the west. Thus the great German offensive of early 1918, which was designed to annihilate the Allied armies and win the war before the manpower of the United States could make itself felt, did not have the divisions that might have made victory possible. In the end Ludendorff's military prestige is diminished because he did not foresee that shortsighted vengeance in the east would cost him everything in the west.

Another analogy can be made between the two treaties. As Versailles, in the beginning, was theoretically to have been based on the idealism of the Fourteen Points, Brest-Litovsk had been preceded by an idealistic "Peace Resolution," offered by the Social Democrats in Germany. And at both peace conferences there were those who were interested only in plunder and revenge; those who voiced their support for principles but voted according to the realities; those who fought for principle to the bitter end and suffered the eternal disappointment of the idealist.

In February 1918 Germany's two conservative parties (Conservatives and National Liberals) approved the terms of Brest-Litovsk. This was hardly surprising, since the political right had consistently supported the cause of war; but surprising indeed was the approval given to the treaty by the parties in the center, the Centrists and the Progressives, who had voted along with the Social Democrats to put through the Peace Resolution of July 1917. The Progressives argued that although they attached great importance to the reestablishment of friendly relations with Russia, they did not believe that this result would be achieved by dealing on equal terms with the Bolsheviks. And Matthias Erzberger, the mercurial Centrist leader, argued that the conditions laid down in the German ultimatum were consistent with the principles proclaimed by the Peace Resolution.

Only the Social Democrats and Independents denounced the German proposals. Philipp Scheidemann, the Social Democrats' most effective orator, flatly asserted that the treatment being accorded the Russians would in the long run be harmful to Germany's best interests. "We are fighting," he said, "to defend our Fatherland, not to destroy Russia." He warned that revolution would be the consequence of failure to conclude a just peace, and that due to her annexationist policy, Germany was losing her last friends abroad.

Scheidemann made his plea during the debate on the terms of the German ultimatum. The terms had been told to the Reichstag on February 26, 1918; on February 28 the Soviet delegation arrived in Brest-Litovsk, and three days later the treaty was signed. The efforts of the Social Democrats to modify the terms had been in vain. When the treaty was presented to the Reichstag for ratification, the Social Democrats, instead of voting against the annexations, abstained. They justified their behavior by arguing that to vote against the peace treaty would be to vote in favor of prolonging the war. Only the Independents voted No. An Independent spokesman, Hugo Haase, said: "It is very easy, in time of peace, when there is no question of coming to a decision, to speak out in purely theoretical fashion against a policy of violence. But it is the special duty of those who are sincere about this to make themselves heard when the principle involved is being put to a practical test. . . ."

The spirit of Brest-Litovsk prepared the way for the so-called Peace of Paris in 1919. The same worldwide malaise pervaded both agreements, for it would soon be apparent that the First

World War left more than a legacy of physical death and suffering. A war fought on so vast a scale around the world over a period of so many years had to leave behind a legacy of moral or spiritual decline; soon it became evident that there was an increasing indifference to the taking of life, an acceptance of violence as a way of conducting human affairs. No student of the times thinks that the violence of the 1920's, the gang wars in the cities of the United States, was due solely to the fact that Prohibition was enacted during the war. A cynicism, a disbelief in justice and other moral values of the prewar age, was part of the atmosphere of the world, but most particularly in America and Europe.

In the nations which had been defeated, a kind of hysterical rage built up and was nurtured by the economic depression that introduced the phenomena of breadlines and soup kitchens. There was a casting about for a scapegoat, and it is reasonable to ascribe to this the revival of anti-Semitism, similar in so many ways to the outbreaks of witch-burning that came after the Thirty Years' War.

This sickness was exacerbated by the partitioning of the world. (When the United Nations was founded in 1945 fifty countries were represented; in less than a generation membership increased almost 150 percent, and the Secretary-General, U Thant, was issuing a pitiful appeal against the creation of any more "ministates." One member state of the United Nations is the island of Barbados, population 242,000 and area 166 square miles.) The beginning of this partitioning could be seen back in the days of 1918 in the idealists' drive for "self-determination" of individual peoples and the cold-blooded cynicism of more practical politicians.

Thus was created the brand-new republic of Czechoslovakia, which included three and a half million Germans (to whom Adolf Hitler is later to turn his attention), and somewhat smaller blocs of Ukrainians and Hungarians. The new state of Yugoslavia was made up of a potpourri of Serbs, Croats, Slovenes, Montenegrins, Albanians, and Macedonians. Rumania, besides Rumanians, had a populace comprised of Bulgarians, more Ukrainians and Hungarians, Serbs and Germans, and independent Poland included Germans, Russians, Lithuanians, and, of course, Ukrainians.

These new states, in the true Balkan tradition, were instantly at each other's throats, refusing to trade with each other even when it would have been to their mutual advantage and using their resources to try to damage their neighbors rather than to help themselves. Nowhere was the cynicism of the great powers more obvious than here. The principle of the self-determination of small nations was invoked only (1) when it served the Allies' military aims or (2) where it would hurt the enemy or (3) where the interests of international banking were served profitably. Self-determination was denied Ireland because its neutrality during the war conflicted with the first purpose; it was denied Bulgaria because it conflicted with the second, and to East Galicia because it conflicted with the third.

Sir Norman Angell asked:

> In other words, do Americans seriously argue that the moral forces which have wrought such havoc in the foreign policy of European states could never threaten the foreign policy of America? I suggest that if an English government can be led to sanction and defend in Ireland the identical things which shocked the world when committed in Belgium by Germans, if France today threatens Europe with a military hegemony not less mischievous than that which America determined to destroy, the causes of those things must be sought, not in the special wickedness of this or that nation, but in forces which may operate among any people. It is precisely the truth which Americans today are refusing to face. We all admit that "human nature being what it is," preponderance of power, irresponsible power is something which no nation (but our own) can be trusted to use wisely or with justice. The backbone of American policy shall therefore be an effort to retain preponderance of power. If this be secured little else matters. . . .

And John Maynard Keynes commented:

> The proceedings of Paris all had this air of extraordinary importance and unimportance at the same time. The decisions seemed charged with consequences to the future of

> human society; yet the air whispered that the word was not flesh, that it was futile, insignificant, of no effect, dissociated from events; and one felt most strongly the impression, described by Tolstoy in *War and Peace* or by Hardy in *The Dynasts,* of events marching on to their conclusion uninfluenced and unaffected by the cerebrations of Statesmen in Council. . . .

Wilson, Keynes felt, was "not sensitive to his environment at all. What chance could such a man have against Mr. Lloyd George's unerring, almost medium-like, sensibility to everyone immediately round him?"

Wilson indeed seemed to be acting the role of a Presbyterian minister, thus confirming the judgment of those advisers who urged him to stay in Washington during the peace conference. His influence would have been greater, the advisers felt, if his Secretary of State did the arguing in Paris, and he would have been able to think more clearly away from the diplomatic debates. A formidable array of these advisers (Herbert Hoover, Bernard Baruch, Colonel House, Secretary of State Robert Lansing) made this argument, but Wilson was already embarked on the headstrong course that was to mark the end of his career with tragedy.

Clemenceau emerged as the most formidable man at the conference table. Most observers felt that by and large the members of the French delegation offered the largest number of proposals, which Clemenceau often modified—hence, his reputation as a moderate. But that is an oversimplification of the French purpose. The French had come to the conference table with the knowledge that they had won the war (with help) and they were determined to emasculate Germany. Their initial proposals were always extreme, and the American and British negotiators finally came to be embarrassed about the amount of pleading that they were doing for the German point of view. So, as the conference went on, more and more often it was Clemenceau's "moderation" that broke a threatened stalemate.

All of Clemenceau's proposals, of course, however "moderate," had but one aim in view: to insure that France would be so strong and Germany so weak that never again would Germany dare attack. A peace based on the Fourteen Points alone had no place at all in Clemenceau's thinking, though Wilson remained unaware of this. France's essential plan for dealing with Germany was precisely what Germany's had been for dealing with Russia: to reduce Germany's population by reducing her territory; to reduce her military power by disbanding her armies and navies, and to reduce her economic capabilities by demanding reparations. Emotionally, Clemenceau was ideally suited to engineer such a program, for his feelings about the Germans were that the Hun is either under your heel or at your throat. Clemenceau believed that the German understood nothing but force, that in negotiation there is no advantage he would not take, that he was without honor, pride, or mercy. It was impossible to conciliate a German, Clemenceau believed, for he regarded that as an admission of weakness; you must dictate to him. Naturally, Clemenceau did not make a public parade of these convictions. Later, in his writings, he made this clear, along with his contempt for "sentimentality" in international relations, his belief that the politics of power were eternal and inevitable, and his judgment of the Americans as naïve, the British as hypocritical.

For all his perceptions, because he interpreted World War I as simply the most recent chapter in the war-scarred history of Franco-German relations, Clemenceau was finally no less myopic than Lloyd George, preoccupied with remaining in power at home, or Wilson, obsessed with the notion of insuring justice for all but unmindful of the diminution of his power at home and his prestige in Europe.

# IV

## NEW FORCES IN THE WEST

The old order changeth
yielding place to new.
Tennyson

THE DISRUPTION OF THE class system, an irreparable rent in the fabric of prewar Europe, was not at first noticed: no comparable disruption had occurred in European history since the decline of feudalism. Artists and intellectuals particularly were affected. In times of upheaval, when society is absorbed primarily by the struggle for material recovery, cultural activity is one of the first things to go under. In the process the material bases of learning and culture are undermined: the expense of printed materials increases enormously, as do the costs of paint, canvas, and marble; even the circulation of books and magazines may be curtailed because of differences in the value of national currencies.

The changes were early manifest in the decline of the educational system in Europe. In Russia education, art, science, and every other phase of intellectual activity were converted into tools of propaganda. European intellectuals or, more precisely, its educated, lost the respect they had held before the war. "Now what is to be the outcome of conditions in which the profiteer sets the social tone; in which lamplighters and streetcleaners are paid better than teachers and professors?" asked one critic, who also wondered: "When the present generation of intellectuals, today decimated by privation or even abandoning their callings, is gone, who will take their place?"

Things didn't turn out quite as badly as that—such true intellectuals as Bertrand Russell managed to keep their reputations, but there is no doubt that the class of teachers and writers was hard hit by the war; besides the evils endured by all others, these people were exposed to certain ills peculiar to themselves. "To enter their homes is to witness not merely physical want and decline of material living standards, but also mental and spiritual starvation and destruction of cherished ideals—tragedies, which, in this case, are even harder to be borne," it was pointed out.

These people are a "class" in a sense quite different from other social groups, for within this class there is greater variety—differences of origin, economic status, activities, and outlook. Nonetheless, an "intellectual international" had existed in Europe before the war. There was a consciousness, a kind of unity among intellectuals, that transcended national boundaries, and this intellectual unity was shattered by the war.

Changes were also overtaking the aristocracy. Even before the war, a divisive process began that separated the traditional landed aristocracy from the newer, financial-industrial plutocracy. In Western Europe, before the war, the financial-industrial plutocracy had begun to move steadily into the ascendant. Money, simply as money, became increasingly important as a measure of social status. Land, or the ownership of land, had previously been the measure of importance (and may be again as the population of the world marches on its apparently irreversible way), but generally land is not an investment that increases in value at the rate of even the least rewarding of business enterprises. Industries that returned the greatest rate of riches—railroads in those days, for example, or steel or textile mills—made their entrepreneurs wealthy, their riches exceeding by far that of the great landowners. Wealth, wherever it existed, has always been able to create its own aristocracy. Especially was this true in England where royal pragmatists deliberately made wealthy businessmen part of the existing aristocracy, creating the "beer barons" and the "press lords."

Across the continent, the aristocracy as a whole declined as a political power during and after World War I. The reigning houses of Russia, Germany, and Austria-Hungry were all driven from power in postwar revolutions. However, the aristocracy was still able to hold its own in some nations because the revolution in Russia and the attempted revolutions in Germany raised the new specter of communism. In Hungary, for example, an alliance of peasants and aristocrats defeated the communist republic of Bela Kun; and in Germany the industrialists and the bankers deserted the deposed Hohenzollerns and cast their lot, for a time, with the new republic.

In Europe the aristocracy was disappearing not only because so many of its sons had been killed, nor even because the "beer barons" were elbowing the traditional aristocracy aside, but because the very concept of aristocracy no longer had a valid meaning. The function of the aristocracy had been to supply an elite executive corps for the monarchies—the ambassadors, the army officers, the managers, the financial men, the administrators. In the newly born republics where before the war the aristocracy had been an alien ruling class, there was now no place for them. The aristocracy, however, never succumbed to the bourgeois acceptance of the Protestant ethic that equated a man's worth with his wealth, and if members of the aristocracy were no longer wanted as ministers of state, they could with some equanimity go into business or even—as in Paris, London, or New York—take pride in becoming nightclub doormen, headwaiters, or even taxi drivers, not to mention such other rewarding careers as fortune-hunting or memoir-writing. (It is interesting to note that one of the reasons for the continuation of the secret police in Russia, besides the tradition of the Czars and the immutable conviction of conspirators that they are being conspired against, was that the new masters of the state had not themselves the capacity to run it. Especially in industry, for example, the mill managers had to be those chosen by the Czars, at least until new managers could be trained.)

In addition, shortages and standardization of available foods contributed to the process of communizing social experience and telescoping class. Such food innovations as haricot-bean fritters, "savory" oatmeal pudding, barley rissoles, and nut rolls, were devised for those middle- and upper-class households accustomed in prewar days to the first and largest claim to good foods and prime meats. Now under state-directed distribution these items began to find their way into poorer homes, and price control made them purchasable by the lowliest housewives.

During the war, other developments further reduced the privileges of class. For the first time, taxation became a serious burden to the landed gentry, and for the first time businessmen moved into the political elite, as Lloyd George appointed them in measurable numbers to ministerial posts. This new recruitment, outside the aristocracy, of government offices coincided with the wartime extension of the powers and functions of government, in turn further bolstered by the prestige which businessmen had acquired in this new war of machines and industrial systems. Now, too, came the rise of the Labour party.

The top hats and butterfly collars that had marked the upper-class gentlemen were disappearing, and the rationing of gasoline was making the small car popular.

A great undefined egalitarian movement seemed to be sweeping the world in 1918. In Britain, the Representation of the People Act was passed in 1918, which gave political recognition not only to women (women householders and the wives of householders got the vote provided they were over thirty) but also to the working classes, for the vote was also given to men over twenty-one. (The 19th amendment to the U. S. Constitution, also giving the vote to women, would become law in 1920.) A good part of this was undoubtedly due to the war. Although officers and men had served under like terms in the American Civil War, the true forerunner of twentieth-century warfare, this had not been true in Europe until World War I. Now the mass-circulation newspapers invented the kind of war correspondent who found more colorful copy in the stories of the individual soldiers than in the changing of battle lines on the war maps at general headquarters, and the Tommy and the poilu came into his own as much as Haig and Foch. While the Tommy and the poilu—and the doughboy—were being hailed as the saviors of their countries on the battlefield, at home the munitions factories and the government offices were giving jobs to women who otherwise would have sensibly remained at home.

Oddly enough, in England royalty got a boost up while it was collapsing everywhere else; while all the royal houses of Europe were falling, one powerful Emperor alone survived the ruin, George V, although in Italy Victor Emmanuel and in Spain Alfonso XIII continued to hold power. It seemed a miracle that the once-tiny house of Coburg endured as the royal houses of

Hapsburg, Hohenzollern, and Romanov passed on. During the war the English Coburgs changed their name, though the majority of their subjects didn't know it. (At the same time the Coburg Hotel became the Connaught.)

The changes cut by the war in the fabric of society became eminently apparent when contrasted with the society that existed before the war—the Edwardian society, which above all seemed immutable. The goods produced by the Industrial Revolution were there for all to see and most to enjoy. Along with the abundance of goods to use and to trade, the Industrial Revolution eased travel and increased leisure. The working class called forth by the new industrial system was regarded as basically peasants taken from the fields and put to work in the cities—as indeed much of it was. But the relocated peasant soon discovered a powerful weapon to ease his plight, the strike. Striking workers, could —and, in time, would—close down the factories and in the end affect the entire economy. World War I, the first total industrial war of the world, gave furious impetus to those changes.

The working class grew and prospered. Miners, munitions workers, mechanics, and technicians, all vastly improved their lot. Professional men, particularly the lawyers, had also done much better. Lawyers had a field day with the Defense of the Realm Act in Britain and with the proliferation of wartime emergency regulations in the United States. This was also the first major war in which special government bureaus were set up (the start of true bureacracy) to handle activities that had no peacetime counterpart—gas rationing and railroad regulation, to cite but two. Lawyers drew the framework of these departments, so naturally other lawyers would have to guide them.

As the professional middle class began to take on the strength that characterizes them even to this day, the aristocracy and the petty bourgeois began to lessen in comparative importance. One sociologist wrote:

> The middle class was destroyed in Russia. In Central Europe it is withering away; in Western Europe it is staggering under crushing burdens. It was threatened before World War I by the increasing concentration of capital in

> the hands of the few great financial or industrial magnates. Also, taxes kept rising, and so did the cost of living. Even then, nevertheless, the middle class was still prosperous and politically powerful. Moreover, they had a sense of their own importance. Then came the war. The middle class made the greatest sacrifices, then had nothing to show for their efforts. They form the "New Poor" in Central Europe. They began to organize. The organization took two forms: (1) The Middle Classes Union (M.C.U.) in Britain, founded in 1919, and the Civic Union of France, founded in 1920; and (2) the Fascists who came to power in Italy in 1922, a middle-class reaction to communist extremism in the face of a seriously disrupted economic picture.

It was, of course, in Germany that the middle classes were hardest hit. During the war, the mark had been seriously deflated, but by November of 1921, a dollar was worth 200 marks and two years later a dollar was worth 4 billion marks. It is almost impossible today to comprehend the extremes of that inflation. An ordinary postage stamp cost 12 million marks, a newspaper 200 million. The mark as a medium of exchange had no meaning. As Taylor points out in *The Fall of the Dynasties:*

> This terrible inflation wrought havoc to the Protestant ethic of the middle class. Those who had practiced thrift, prudence, and life-long self-restraint found themselves ruined. Meanwhile, some people who had gambled, squandered, and borrowed beyond their means grew rich overnight. As their faith in the traditional values associated with money-making was destroyed, the middle class lost a great part of their trust not only in government, but in society, in God, in the basic decencies of life itself. The shock was aggravated by the downfall of the traditional symbols of authority. In postwar Germany the impoverished middle class was threatened by starvation. This danger was eventually to pass, but the loss of self-respect involved left permanent damage: it caused many members of the middle class (or former middle class) to turn savage and give Hitler the mass following he needed

to convert his lunatic-fringe movement into a revolutionary menace.

To the people of Germany, the bitter fact of the Empire's defeat seemed unreal. Only a few months earlier the German army had been at the height of its power; General Ludendorff's spring offensive had advanced the German line to within forty miles of Paris. Victory had seemed so close. Then, when the tide turned and the Allies began to force the German retreat, the truth was kept from the German nation. No one knew of the desperate situation until suddenly the nearly "victorious" Germany was suing for peace.

The situation was indeed desperate and continued resistance would have been suicidal, but the German people did not know this. At the very moment the armistice was signed, indeed, the German army was still fighting outside Germany's frontiers and still held an unbroken front in the west. So, the terms which the Allied nations were to exact of the new republic seemed particularly harsh. If these terms had been exacted from an invaded, destroyed Germany, they would have been understandable, but this army was undefeated. A betrayal by the politicians seemed the only explanation for Germany's humiliation, and the new republic was to become the logical scapegoat.

In signing the armistice, the leaders of the German Republic were also signing their own political death warrants. (This was physically true of Matthias Erzberger, the chairman of the Armistice Commission and head of the Catholic Center, who was assassinated in August of 1921 by members of the nationalist right.) But to these new leaders of Germany, no other alternative was open. The tide had turned against Germany in July when the Allies halted the Germans' attempt to cross the Marne; other Allied triumphs followed in quick succession, and these victories were soon followed by the collapse of Germany's partners—Austria-Hungary, Bulgaria, and Turkey. Now inferior in numbers, armaments, and equipment, Germany—although she still appeared strong—was left no choice but to accept the Allies' terms for an armistice.

Because Germany was still a young nation in the family of

nations, the developments of the First World War and the years immediately following were probably especially confusing. Once a small collection of states in the center of Europe, periodically invaded from almost every direction, Germany was not forged into a single modern state till the middle of the nineteenth century. The conquering Romans had not given the same sense of law and order to the Huns that they had to the Gauls and to other Mediterranean peoples, and even Christianity had come late to the Germans. Neither had Germany ever had a revolution in the sense that France had, nor even one like the "hidden revolution" of the British.

It is true that Germany gave the world the Reformation, but the Reformation divided Germany more than ever and led directly to the Thirty Years' War (1618 to 1648), which left the German states devastated and depopulated, reduced almost to impotence.

Briefly the House of Hohenzollern pushed east from Prussia and built a powerful military state under Frederick the Great, but Prussia, too, succumbed to the all-conquering Napoleon in the early nineteenth century. Not for another half century was Germany to become a united nation, under the reign of the "Iron Chancellor" Otto von Bismarck and the Prussian Junkers, a unity forged of blood and iron. On January 18, 1871, during the siege of Paris, the "German Empire" was proclaimed at Versailles.

"At last," points out one historian,

> "the Germanies," or part of them, became "Germany." . . . The new *Reich,* inspired by a young patriotism which was military and semi-feudal in its content and expression, was thus belatedly launched upon its brilliant career. Just as German *Kultur* has ever been an unstable amalgam of conflicting forces and inner contradictions, so German politics and diplomacy have often exhibited the marks of internal disunity and collective consciousness of inferiority, induced by long subservience to the more mature and powerful communities to the west and south. The patriots of the Hohenzollern Empire appeared often to be fierce and fanatical in their devotion to the Fatherland precisely because they were,

within themselves, unsure of their loyalty and uncertain of the true unity and worth of the long-divided nation which they loved.

Strangely, it was the young Wilhelm II, who dismissed Bismarck as chancellor, who led Germany into the bloody international struggle for colonies and power. Germany's aggressive quest for a "place in the sun" was in part a drive to prove that she was the equal of the other nations of the West; the blunders of her diplomats and the mistakes of her generals were due more to this desperate drive for a respected place as a leader among nations and an ignorance of the behavior of nations rather than to stupidity. But in the end the results were the same.

When the war broke out in August 1914, the leaders of Germany's Social Democratic party, the nation's largest popular party, abandoned their traditional pacifist principles and voted funds for the war effort. The overwhelming majority of the German people then believed that the war had been thrust upon the Fatherland by jealous and vindictive neighbors, that Germany had never wanted this war, and that she was fighting to save herself from destruction. Because most Social Democrats were Germans first and Socialists second, they shared this feeling. They remained as opposed as ever to imperialistic enterprises, to ventures undertaken for territorial or economic gain. But, to the Social Democrats, this war was different. It was a war in defense of the Fatherland against outside aggression, especially Russian aggression. Always, there had been an almost pathological fear of Russia, and all Germans were convinced that defeat in this war would mean that German women and children would fall prey to Russian bestiality. It would mean ruin for every German, regardless of class. Therefore, the Social Democratic declaration of August 4 concluded: "We will not desert our Fatherland in this hour of peril. . . . We . . . condemn all wars of aggression. We demand that, directly our security is won and our enemies are inclined to make peace, the war should end in a peace that will make friendly relations with neighbors possible."

The Social Democrats were in earnest when they said they wanted a just peace. Throughout the war, they demanded the unequivocal repudiation of all annexationist designs. But as time went on, dissatisfaction and unrest within the party grew, as the dictatorial rule of the nation by the Supreme Command and the pursuit of annexationist dreams became fixed.

Erich Ludendorff, First Quartermaster General under Field Marshal Paul von Hindenburg, became virtual dictator of Germany. He was no man to worry about the fortunes or the feelings of the mass of the people; his people were the landowners and the industrialists. In early 1917, in opposition to Ludendorff, a minority of the Social Democrats took a hard stand against the war and split from the party, calling themselves the Independent Social Democrats.

But the regular Social Democrats, as well as the more moderate Catholic Centrists, soon came to join the Independents in opposition to the war. A speech by the Centrist leader, Matthias Erzberger, in the Reichstag on July 6, 1917, precipitated the crisis. Erzberger had been a rabid annexationist, but by now he had completely changed his mind and had come to the conclusion that only by seeking a moderate peace could Germany save herself. The entry of the United States into the war in April 1917 had darkened Germany's chances of ultimate victory. The radical elements in Russia and the socialist parties in Germany were scoring heavy political gains with their slogan: No annexations, no indemnities. The national will to fight was weakening. The defection of Austria-Hungary was clearly coming.

Against this ominous backdrop Erzberger announced his conversion to the idea of a just peace. The picture he painted was unrelievedly black. He called attention to the staggering financial cost of the war. He enlarged upon the steadily worsening food situation. Unrestricted submarine warfare, he warned, would fail to accomplish its purpose. Continuation of the war would lead to ruin. It was necessary to go back to the mood of August 1914: The best way to obtain peace was to reaffirm what had been declared to be her just purpose at the beginning of the conflict, that she was fighting a solely defensive war, that she wanted a just peace in which no nation would be oppressed. This, Erzberger said, the Reichstag should say to the German Government; it would then be up to the chancellor to make diplomatic use of the statement.

There was no need to bother about the 25,000 pan-Germans. Let them go crazy, Erzberger jeered. It would be cheaper to build asylums for them than to prolong the war.

But Reich Chancellor Theobald von Bethmann-Hollweg was not in sympathy with Erzberger's views, and now the Centrists, the Social Democrats, and the Progressives resolved to drive him from office. They coupled their goal of a just peace with a program of constitutional reform. Von Bethmann-Hollweg made concessions, but he was not prepared to go as far as this group wanted, especially in view of the harsh criticism he was getting from the parties of the right—the Conservatives and the National Liberals—and finally von Bethmann-Hollweg was forced to submit his resignation to the Emperor. The Emperor, despite the crisis in the Reichstag, failed to consult the delegates in appointing a successor. His choice was a lackluster bureaucrat, Dr. Georg Michaelis, food commissioner for Prussia.

This error in tactics emboldened the Reichstag to return insult for injury. On July 19, 1917, the Peace Resolution was introduced. Adopted by a majority composed of Social Democrats, Centrists, and Progressives, the resolution ran as follows:

> As on August 4, 1914, the words of the speech from the throne, "No desire for conquest urges us forward," hold good for the German people now, as the beginning of the fourth year of war. Germany has taken up arms in defense of her freedom and independence and for the integrity of her territory. The object of the Reichstag is to obtain a peace of understanding and of lasting reconciliation between nations. With such a peace, forced cessions of territory and political, economic, and financial oppression are incompatible. The Reichstag rejects all plans that may entail an economic boycott and foster hostile feelings among the nations after the war. The freedom of the seas must be definitely established. Only harmony in economic matters will prepare the ground for a friendly concord among nations. The Reichstag will energetically sponsor the creation of international courts of arbitration. However, so long as the enemy governments do not entertain such a peace, so long as they threaten Germany

> and her allies with territorial seizures and violence, the German people will stand together as one man, will hold on unshaken and fight till their own right and that of their allies to live and develop have been secured. The German people are unconquerable when united. The Reichstag knows it has the concurrence of the men who are heroically defending the Fatherland. The everlasting gratitude of the entire nation is assured them.

The Reichstag's action was a slap in the face for the Supreme Command; Ludendorff had tried hard to prevent adoption of the resolution, but his objections were swept aside. Parliament's declaration of independence was to have grave consequences, for it made dramatically clear how the course of the war, the endless casualties without victory, was straining the political fabric of the state. The declaration effectively ended the political unity that had been established in 1914 and made clear that the Junkers, without military triumphs, were losing control of the government.

By September of 1918 it had become apparent to the German High Command, including the General Staff—and most particularly including Ludendorff and Paul von Hindenburg—that the war had been lost. On the 29th of September, Ludendorff and von Hindenburg told the Kaiser not only that the military situation was so bad that he must ask for an armistice as quickly as possible, but also that the political situation had deteriorated to such an extent—as evidenced by the action of the Reichstag—that the only way in which he could maintain his throne was by what they called a revolution from above: by the granting of concessions and the establishment of a parliamentary monarchy. The Kaiser at length consented. The chancellor, Count Georg von Hertling, resigned, and on October 3 Prince Max of Baden became the first "democratic" chancellor of Germany. Prince Max was a Prussian major-general and the heir to a grand duchy but he had also earned a reputation as a "liberal." He now offered a series of political reforms, but he was too late; the military disintegration was overtaking the political, and the High Command, anxious to save the nucleus of an effective military power, demanded that peace negotiations be initiated at once. The home front was holding up, the armies were still fighting, but at general headquarters in Spa in occupied Belgium, morale was gone. Prince Max was obliged to open negotiations with Wilson, who considered the establishment of a republic a prerequisite to peace. This, of course, enraged the entire Prussian officer corps, and they preferred to go on fighting rather than accept any such condition. Wilson, however, did not stick to the point, and finally the Cabinet was able to agree to the conditions that were laid down.

But now a new point arose. Most of the leaders of Germany recognized that to the world—and indeed to Germany itself—the Kaiser had become the symbol of the whole vast bloody struggle of the war, and either by revolution internally or by pressure externally, he would have to go. These same leaders were deeply concerned that any violent change in the government would also end the dynasty. Only the Kaiser's abdication could save the situation. Prince Max, Friedrich Ebert, Philipp Scheidemann, and other leaders of the Social Democratic party urged upon General Wilhelm Gröner, who had succeeded Ludendorff after the Kaiser forced the latter's resignation, the necessity of the Kaiser's abdication to preserve a parliamentary monarchy to be headed by one of the Kaiser's sons. Gröner and von Hindenburg would not listen to the politicians and so, through their stubborn insistence on trying to keep things as they were, it turned out to be the generals who brought down the Kaiser, the dynasty, the government, and the Emperor.

The so-called revolution in Germany toward the end of 1918 was no revolution at all in the true sense. Rather it was a series of events that occurred as desperate men tried to improvise a government in the political vacuum of a collapsing nation, the hurricane of absolute defeat in a dreadful war screaming around them. A typical event was the naval meeting at Kiel on November 4, provoked by a lunatic plan of the officers to steam out in a final suicide attack on the British Navy. Two days later an armistice delegation, headed by the Centrist leader Matthias Erzberger, left Berlin to sign a truce with Foch.

Event on event followed fast. An uprising in Munich put the revolutionist Kurt Eisner in the presidency of a "peasants, workers, and soldiers' council," and the 800-year-old Wittelsbach dynasty—far older than the Hohenzollerns—fell, and was replaced by the short-lived Bavarian republic. On November 8, the Social Democrats in the Cabinet in Berlin resigned because of the Kaiser's refusal to abdicate. Wilhelm countered by proposing that he, personally, would lead the army against the "traitors" at home, but the generals had to inform him that now the army would probably not fight.

Wilhelm proposed finally to abdicate as Kaiser but not as King of Prussia. However, it was now too late for even that. The following day the crown council, including von Hindenburg, advised him to abdicate; and Prince Max, without authorization, publicly announced the abdication.

Much of the reasoning behind the urging of the Kaiser to abdicate had come from the absolute insistence of Woodrow Wilson that it must be done. By late October Wilson was writing:

> . . . significant and important as the constitutional changes seem to be which are spoken of by the German Foreign Secretary in his note of 20th October, it does not appear that the principle of a government responsible to the German people has yet been fully worked out, or that any guarantees exist or are in contemplation that the alterations of principle and of action now partially agreed upon will be permanent.
>
> Moreover, it does not appear that the heart of the present difficulty has been reached. It may be that future wars have been brought under the control of the German people; but the present war has not been; and it is with the present war that we are dealing. It is evident that the German people have no means of commanding the acquiescence of the military authorities of the Empire in the popular will; that the power of the King in Prussia to control the policy of the Empire is unimpaired, that the determining initiative still remains with those who have hitherto been the masters of Germany.
>
> Feeling that the whole peace of the world depends now on plain speaking and straightforward action, the President deems it his duty to say, without any attempt to soften what

> may seem harsh words, that the nations of the world do not and cannot trust the word of those who have hitherto been the masters of German policy, and to point out once more that in concluding peace and attempting to undo the infinite injuries and injustices of this war, the Government of the United States cannot deal with any but veritable representatives of the German people, who have been assured of a genuine constitutional standing as the real rulers of Germany. If it must deal with the military masters and the monarchical autocrats of Germany now, or if it is likely to have to deal with them later in regard to the international obligations of the German Empire, it must demand, not peace negotiations but surrender. Nothing can be gained by leaving this essential thing unsaid.

It was against the background of diplomatic correspondence such as this that Germany's leaders were trying to act. The choice lay between keeping the Kaiser or ending the war. And if they chose to keep the Kaiser, they not only would be beaten on the field of battle, but also would almost certainly face years of military occupation.

It is impossible even now to assess the full effect of Wilson's words, for they not only dismayed the Germans who had to deal with them immediately, they reverberated through every country that had a monarchy, and there is no estimating how many antiroyalists took them as a license to rise against their own crowned heads and demand the establishment of a democracy, in line with the wishes of the President of the United States. There was an outburst of rage and despair among the monarchists, who saw in the Wilson statement "an attempt to deliver Germany from the Hohenzollern," "an endeavor to put an end to the monarchic system." The Empress Auguste Victoria herself spoke of "the audacity of the parvenu across the seas who has thus dared to humiliate a princely house." And it was not simply royalty and monarchists who were appalled; the agrarian paper *Deutsche Tageszeitung* protested this "most intolerable outrage" with the question: "Must they not think a people capable of the depths of treason when they expect it to abandon a dynasty which has been the architect of its greatness throughout the course of a glorious history?"

Nonetheless, the abdication was inevitable. After Wilson's note, the forces demanding the Kaiser's departure began to gather ever-increasing strength. There had to be peace, war could no longer be abided, and while few had actually thought ahead to what might follow, there was now a lot of public talk about abdication. The most universal rumor in Germany was that abdication would mean milder peace terms and the forestallment of invasion and occupation of Germany. Abdication, it was believed, would be used as a bargaining counter with the Allies. As the days and the weeks dragged by and the death list grew, more and more Germans began to ask for and then to demand the abdication of Wilhelm II who was now becoming the symbol of continuing a futile, endless combat. The Social Democrat Philipp Scheidemann, who later became chancellor, wrote: "If the war had ended in the victory of Germany, the Emperor would have been exalted beyond all measure. He would probably have become little less than a demigod. Since events turned out otherwise, a scapegoat was looked for and was found in the Kaiser." In the closing days of October and the opening ones of November, it seemed that nothing was talked about in Germany—outside of the war, of course—except the abdication. It was all that was heard on the trains, on the sidewalks, in the cafés, and on the trolleys.

Undoubtedly abdication was the thought farthest from the mind of the Kaiser, even though Prince Max, heir to the throne of Baden and a close relative of Wilhelm II, had for weeks been urging him to abdicate in favor of his twelve-year-old grandson, Wilhelm. Prince Max reasoned that the Allies might agree to a constitutional monarchy if the monarch were a young boy, free of the stain of war guilt, and so the Hohenzollerns might continue to rule. Much later, Prince Max commented:

> I am still convinced that before the evening of 8 November, and even well into the forenoon of 9 November, before the mass of the people had sallied out into the streets, if the Kaiser had followed the way of safety which I had pointed

> out to him, we should have neither the Revolution, nor the Republic of the Workers' Council, nor the murder of Matthias Erzberger. I should have been able to lead Germany into the way of peace. The reforms achieved by my government would have been safeguarded, and Germany could have developed her reforms without breaking with the past. . . .

He may have been right. Certainly, when he traveled to Berlin on October 1 to assume the duties of chancellor, he carried with him plans for reform that were in accord with his reputation as a man dedicated to democracy. But by then it was too late for plans. An early abdication, say in mid-October, might—but only might—have saved the monarchy by convincing the West and particularly Woodrow Wilson that Germany was willing to make fundamental political changes: to become, perhaps not a republic or a democracy, but a constitutional monarchy. Even if that aim had failed, the early abdication almost certainly would have demonstrated to the German people themselves the extent of political changes anticipated and might have headed off the riots and bloodshed that were to mark the years after the war. Whether it might even have prevented the Nazis from eventually gaining power is far too dreamlike to consider.

Prince Max's plans were made suspect by the fact of his being a prince; and in the midst of war a program for constitutional reform is hardly likely to capture the popular imagination. Indeed, it is highly unlikely that the average German of that month, much less the average American, realized how important were the changes that brought Prince Max to power, much less the importance of the changes he intended to make. The abdication might have changed all that. The uprising that came in November came in part because many people, especially the mutinous sailors, were convinced that Germany was still ruled by the same old clique.

For all his faults, Woodrow Wilson showed enormous courage in trying to get a negotiated peace of any kind, since both his allies abroad (who were wary of idealism of any sort) and his Republican enemies at home, headed by Theodore Roosevelt and Henry

Cabot Lodge (who distrusted Democrats as much as they did foreigners), were united in their opposition to negotiation. To further complicate the problem, public opinion in all the Allied countries refused to believe that the new German Government meant the destruction of the Junker military class and made it clear that they looked on Prince Max's peace appeal as a trick for sowing dissension among Germany's enemies. Wilson had to make concessions to this kind of thinking by taking the hard line: the Germans would have to accept the Fourteen Points without reservation; they must evacuate all occupied territories; they must immediately abandon submarine warfare; and they must give guarantees that the new German Government was a trustworthy negotiating partner by eliminating all autocratic influences—which, of course, meant the abdication of the Kaiser.

Though he did not formally abdicate until November 28, the Kaiser boarded his train in Spa at dawn on November 10 and began the melancholy ride to Holland and to exile. The House of Hohenzollern reigned no more. On November 11 the world war ended with the signing of the armistice in the forest near Compiègne.

For at least a generation, Germany was to suffer for the way in which the war ended. With the Kaiser gone and the fighting done, most of the lesser princes and nobles, frightened at the possibility of a bloodbath, fled the country, and so reverence for nobility, long ingrained in the German character, began to fade. The Junkers, who should have been in total disgrace, were not: Wilhelm and the nobility, by fleeing, brought the blame for the disaster on themselves. Indeed, in the years following the war a myth grew up around Germany's Field Marshal Paul von Hindenberg, who became chief of staff in 1916. Von Hindenberg's popularity derived in part from his 1914 triumph over the Russians at Tannenberg, his early record in the war and, after the war, was enhanced further by his assumption of responsibility for bringing the troops back home. Unlike Ludendorff who fled from the country, von Hindenberg stayed at his post, finished his work and only then retired. In 1925 the German republic elected him as its second president. Under his leadership the republic achieved a larger measure of stability, ratified the Pact of Locarno and entered the League of Nations.

Whether the course of history would have been changed had America, as a nation, recognized what was going on is highly dubious and totally academic; Americans accepted at face value the assertion—made by Woodrow Wilson among others—that Germany was now a republic. But it was a republic doomed almost from the start. For one thing, the government that had accepted defeat (a defeat that most Germans did not comprehend) and that had acquiesced in the peace terms (terms that all Germans thought were cruel, oppressive, and vengeful) was the government of the republic. In addition, few Germans understood democracy in the same terms that Americans understood it. "Democracy," then and now, is essentially an Anglo-Saxon system of politics.

The German—Weimar—Republic, born at a time of deep national bitterness, was headed by the leaders of the Social Democratic party, considered to be the largest, oldest, and most powerful Socialist party in the world. Many of the party members, even in the midst of the changing German situation, did not recognize that the war had swept the old world away. With the war over, they thought that the old world would be reestablished, that soon factories would again be producing consumer goods, that the old jobs would be re-created, and that they would be restored to their old position of speaking for the workers to the bosses. But through the years, while its leaders still talked the slogans of theoretical Marxism, the party itself had become a vast bureaucracy with innumerable ties to the status quo. The party, in short, while theoretically representing the workers of Germany, had made many accommodations with the bosses of Germany. It was no longer to the party's interest to stage any sort of workers' revolution or to establish a German equivalent of the Russian Soviet. In the winter of 1918, therefore, when there were actual uprisings in German cities, the Social Democratic party did not try to forge these minor revolts into a major revolution.

Like Social Democrats the world round, they were anti-Communist. They had seen what had happened in Russia, how the Communists there were subverting the original revolution to their own uses; and they feared that the same thing could happen in Germany. After all, the red flags were already appearing in the towns and the cities where the revolts were breaking out, and many of the uprisings included soldiers and sailors who were bringing guns to the revolution. One of the striking ironies of modern history is that the Communist revolution in Germany was not crushed by the Junkers, but by the Social Democrats.

Crushing the Communists was touch and go for a time, for in 1917 the Social Democrats themselves had split into two factions: the Majority Socialists, led by Friedrich Ebert, and the Independent Socialists, or the radical branch, led by such firebrands as Rosa Luxemburg and Karl Liebknecht. Three of the Majority Socialists, including Ebert, had been named to the Cabinet established by Prince Max. When Max resigned on November 9, at the same time that he announced the abdication of the Kaiser, Ebert took over. In addition, three Independent Socialists were also named to the Cabinet, which now called itself the Council of Peoples Commissars. The council, on November 12, issued a policy paper in which it pledged to establish democracy in Germany (as a word "democracy" was highly regarded in Germany for a number of years) and to establish a number of political reforms which included universal suffrage and proportional representation, the latter a political theory that would not gain any effectiveness even in the United States for another fifty years. Ebert also promised General Gröner that he could "maintain order" in the nation if the military would support him and would demobilize the army as quickly as possible—that move being necessary to get the guns out of the hands of civilian soldiers who had been drafted into the service and who could not be relied on (as the General Staff had informed the Kaiser) to put down civilian uprisings. The precise form of the new government was to be determined by a yet-to-be-elected representative national assembly.

These particular sorts of political reform were not at all to the liking of the extremists of the Independent Socialists, particularly to Rosa Luxemburg and Liebknecht, who now proceeded to form the so-called Spartacist movement, financed in part through the Soviet Embassy, and to demand expropriation of all private property in the name of the slogan "All Power to the Soviets."

If the Americans of that day did not appreciate what was going on in Germany, it was partly that the forces at work were so complicated. Few Americans, for example, knew who Ebert was, apart from his official title and the facts—reported over and over again—that he was fat, the son of a tailor and himself a saddler before his truly remarkable talents as a public speaker, a persuader, and a trade union organizer who had come to the attention of the Social Democrats.

Ebert's decisions were influenced by a number of factors: he had been dealing with splits in his party ever since 1912; he had the nationalistic fear of the Russians—"the barbarians of the East"—that most Germans do; and knowing the German love of aristocracy, he had originally been wedded to the concept of a constitutional monarchy for Germany, provided that the successor to the throne be one of the Kaiser's heirs other than the crown prince. In addition to all this, Ebert had other problems. In April of 1917 the Germans had sent Lenin to Russia in a sealed train to stir up as much mischief as he could in that country; a year later the Russians—the new Russians, the Union of Soviet Socialist Republics—returned the compliment. They sent a new ambassador, Adolf Joffe, to Berlin to stir up as much trouble as he could. He arrived with a staff of three hundred, promptly broke out the banner of the hammer and sickle over the embassy on Unter den Linden, refused to present his credentials to the Kaiser, and invited Luxemburg and Liebknecht to dinner (who were in prison at the time, serving terms for treason and sedition).

Much more than that, he came liberally supplied with money, communist literature, and weapons. By the time the Germans were able to get rid of Joffe by framing him and his staff by planting seditious pamphlets in a railroad station, the damage had been done. Joffe and his staff were expelled on November 7, 1918. But the naval mutiny had broken out in Wilhelmshaven on October 28, and it had spread to the High Seas Fleet in Kiel; revolt was general over north Germany, Munich had been taken by Kurt Eisner's revolutionists, Berlin was crippled by a general strike.

At this juncture the Ebert government took over. The Spartacists and the Russian Communists hoped that Ebert's government could be toppled like Kerensky's, not just because of their belief that the communist revolution was best suited for export to industrial nations, but so that Russia would not be alone in fighting the communist battle to win control of the world. Now it was the Communists' turn to make mistakes.

Joffe had been replaced, following his expulsion, by Karl Radek, and Radek had talked Liebknecht and Rosa Luxemburg into forming a new German Communist party out of the Spartacist movement. This was the first error, for it ineradicably split the left-wing Socialists from the Social Democratic party. In addition, the Spartacist faction urged on a group of sailors (who had been living in the Kaiser's stables in Berlin since November 8, when they had arrived from Kiel to protest the stoppage of their pay) to march on the Chancellery and to occupy it. The sailors cut every telephone line in the Chancellery—except the one that connected Ebert with Gröner. Ebert called for Gröner's troops. The Spartacist rebellion broke out in full force all over Berlin. They were able to gain control of a number of government buildings; general fighting broke out on Christmas Eve, and for a week the government was helpless.

But the Spartacists did not have the strength to follow up. Since the left-wing Independent Socialists had quit the government with the formation of the German Communist party, Ebert had had three posts to fill, including that of War Minister. To this post he had appointed a tough old Social Democrat with no liking for the Communists, Gustav Noske. Noske immediately set about crushing the revolt. "Somebody must be the bloodhound," he said. Noske and his men got considerable help from one of the early Freikorps commanded by a General Staff major, Kurt von Schleicher. "These men," von Schleicher told Ebert and Noske, "know no soldiers' soviets, only their rifles and their captains."

The rise of Freikorps was one of the first signs that Germany was swinging away from the possibility of revolution to a more conservative path. As Ebert tried to steer the country toward general elections for the constituent assembly, signs of a possible civil war grew more ominous. At night handbills reading "Kill the Jews, Kill Liebknecht" appeared on the walls; by day the streets were filled with sound and fury of communist demonstrations. The communist leaders were growing desperate. The revolution had slipped from their hands; the masses of the people were turning elsewhere for leadership. A congress of delegates from the workers' and soldiers' soviets of Germany had voted in favor of convening the Assembly in spite of communist objections, and elections were set for January 19, 1919.

On January 6, 1919, openly encouraged by Radek, communist shock troops in armored cars attempted to storm the Chancellery, while more than 100,000 supporters and sympathizers milled around in Unter den Linden. Detachments of shock troops occupied the Brandenburger Tor, the government printing offices, the railway stations, and a number of barracks. Three hundred Communists invaded the War Office itself, and Liebknecht proclaimed a provisional government. For three days the Reds held power in Berlin. Noske again counterattacked on January 9 with regular troops, armed with howitzers and machine guns. On January 11 some three thousand veteran infantrymen entered the Wilhelmstrasse, and by January 15, Berlin was once more in the hands of the government.

Vengeance was ruthless and instant, and it earned the Defense Minister the nickname of "Mörder" Noske. Liebknecht and Rosa Luxemburg were arrested in the suburbs by officers of the Guard Cavalry Division and brought back to divisional headquarters at the Hotel Eden in Berlin. Rosa Luxemburg was escorted into the Tiergarten, where, it was later proven, she was killed and thrown into the Landwehr Canal. Karl Liebknecht was shot.

The leaderless Communists fought on. The events which took place in Germany between January and May 1919 have been likened to those which put an end to the Paris Commune in the spring of 1871. Wherever communist rioting broke out, the army counterattacked. Germans killed Germans with savage abandon. "No pardon is given," a soldier of the Freikorps wrote his family. "We shoot even the wounded. The enthusiasm is great, almost unbelievable."

Against this background of savagery, the delegates to the National Assembly, which would establish the shape of the new Germany, were elected on January 19, 1919, under the new system of universal sufferage for all men and women over twenty. The Social Democrats got 163 out of a total of 423 delegates—the largest bloc—but this was by no means a majority, so the new government would have to be a coalition. With obvious symbolism, the new government met at Weimar, "the shrine of Goethe, Schiller, and German liberalism." The new constitution was adopted on July 31, and the Assembly moved to Berlin.

How well would the new government work? One historian pointed out:

> The establishment of the Weimar Republic upon firm foundations of belief depended chiefly upon the ability of its leaders to achieve that fusion of nationalistic and democratic loyalties which constitutes the solid underpinning of French, British, and American democracy. In the modern world the middle classes are everywhere and above all patriotic. Where patriotism is identified with liberalism, democratic institutions are secure. Where patriotism is divorced from liberalism in the middle-class mind, democracy necessarily wanes. Could the Weimar Republic enlist the wholehearted allegiance not merely of convinced liberals but of all patriots as well?

As the history of the next twenty years was to demonstrate, the obstacles to achieving this allegiance in war-wracked Germany were insuperable. For almost all Germans of all classes loyalty meant loyalty first to the Kaiser and the Hohenzollerns, to the black, red, and white flag and the eagles of the Empire. Their dreams were of an all-conquering Germany, their memories were of battles fought and battles won. Their ideal was a glittering monarchy, not the drab gray of the Social Democrats. To them the class system of the old Germany was the ordained way of life, not this empty nonsense of the equality of men. Equality of man indeed, when you had but to use your eyes to see that one man lived in a castle and another swept the street.

As for liberalism, to most Germans it meant Wilson and the rest of the foreign conquerers: it was an alien doctrine only a step better than communism; it meant this new world in which they were living where the black, red, and gold banner of a "republic" fluttered over the buildings of a government that had meekly submitted to the terms of their enemies.

In a generation, these feelings might have changed had the Republic become a prosperous and booming nation able presently to regain a position of strength and respect among the nations of the world. But the victors were in no mood to see that happen. From the very beginning the goal was to humiliate Germany, to destroy her. The Treaty of Versailles was hung around her neck like a millstone. The German delegates, of course, were allowed no voice in the deliberations of the Paris Peace Conference. Count Ulrich von Brockdorff-Rantzau, leader of the delegation, was simply given the terms to accept or reject. They were almost intolerable: Germany was to be degraded spiritually by the clauses which found her totally and solely responsible for the war; she was to be rendered impotent by the clauses stripping her of all military power; she was to be ruined economically by the reparations demands; and she was to lose all her colonies, Alsace-Lorraine, the Saar, Malmedy, the Danish borderlands, Danzig, the Polish Corridor, Memel, Upper Silesia, and other territories. The treaty succeeded in uniting the Germans as nothing else could have done; Nationalists and Socialists alike were bitterly opposed to it. But no one would assume responsibility for its rejection. Rejection would have meant invasion by the Allies, occupation—even partition. Germany was incapable of resisting.

"What hand," asked Chancellor Philipp Scheidemann, "would not wither that sought to lay itself and us in those chains?" Scheidemann and von Brockdorff-Rantzau both resigned from the delegation rather than sign the treaty. Scheidemann was succeeded by Chancellor Gustav Bauer on June 20. On June 22 the Weimar Assembly voted to capitulate, 237 to 138, with the condition that the war guilt provision be stricken out. France would accept no conditions and prepared to order her troops to move. The Bauer Cabinet was forced to surrender unconditionally on June 23, and in complete humiliation Foreign Minister Hermann Müller signed the treaty on June 28 in the Hall of Mirrors at Versailles, where the German Empire had been proclaimed forty-eight years earlier.

There was no mercy for the Germans; the German delegates were stoned as they left Paris, and the Allied blockade which condemned hundreds of thousands all over Europe, innocent and guilty alike, to starvation and death, was not lifted until after the treaty had been signed. Germany was excluded from the League of Nations. The democracies had insured that in Germany there would be no democracy.

"I went through a fearful internal struggle," Wilhelm II wrote in his memoirs.

> On the one hand, I, as a soldier, was outraged at the idea of abandoning my still brave, faithful troops. On the other hand, there was the declaration of our foes that they were unwilling to conclude with me any peace endurable to Germany, as well as the statement of my own government that only by my departure for foreign parts was civil war to be prevented. In this struggle I set aside all that was personal. I consciously sacrificed myself and my throne in the belief that, by so doing, I was best serving the interests of my beloved fatherland. The sacrifice was in vain. My departure brought us neither better armistice conditions nor better peace terms; nor did it prevent civil war—on the contrary, it hastened and intensified, in the most pernicious manner, the disintegration in the army and the nation.

Later, Hitler would describe his feelings when the local pastor visited the hospital where he and other soldiers were recuperating and announced to them that "the House of Hohenzollern should no longer bear the German imperial crown; that the fatherland had become a "republic." Unable to suppress his regret at this turn of events, the clergyman tearfully eulogized the royal house, recalling its "services" to Pomerania, Prussia, and to the fatherland. His soldier audience was deeply moved by the old gentleman's account of recent happenings, especially the disclosure that Germany had lost the war.

Hitler's emotions were so stirred that he found it impossible to remain with the group. He "tottered and groped" his way back to his dormitory, and collapsed weeping upon his bunk. ("Since the day when I had stood at my mother's grave, I had not wept.")

His sorrow was compounded by the realization that "it had all been in vain"—all the sacrifices and privations necessitated by war, the suffering, the constant exposure to death.

"Indignation and disgrace" seared Hitler's brow and tormented both his days and his nights, and finally he had to concede to himself that:

> . . . all was lost. Only fools, liars, and criminals could hope in the mercy of the enemy. In these nights hatred grew in me, hatred for those responsible for this deed.
>
> In the days that followed, my own fate became known to me.
>
> I could not help but laugh at the thought of my own future which only a short time before had given me such bitter concern. Was it not ridiculous to expect to build houses on such ground? At last it became clear to me that what had happened was what I had so often feared but had never been able to believe with my emotions.
>
> Kaiser Wilhelm II was the first German Emperor to hold out a conciliatory hand to the leaders of Marxism, without suspecting that scoundrels have no honor. While they still held the imperial hand in theirs, their other hand was reaching for the dagger.
>
> There is no making pacts with Jews; there can only be the hard *either–or.*
>
> I, for my part, decided to go into politics.

Hitler was right in his decision for himself—and even for Germany—for the only future in Germany lay in politics. As a military power, the nation was helpless for the time being. The conditions of the armistice demanded of her the immediate evacuation of all invaded countries and the repatriation of all their inhabitants; as Churchill described it, the surrender in good condition of 5,000 guns, 30,000 machine guns, 2,000 airplanes; evacuation of the left bank of the Rhine; surrender of three bridgeheads on the Rhine; surrender of 5,000 locomotives, 150,000 wagons, 5,000 trucks in good working order (and with spare parts); disclosure of all mines, of delay-action fuses, and assistance in their discovery and destruction; immediate repatriation without reciprocity of all prisoners of war; abandonment of the treaties of Bucharest and Brest-Litovsk; surrendor of six battle cruisers, the best ten battleships, eight light cruisers, fifty of the best destroyers; surrender of all submarines; the right of the Allies on failure of execution of any condition to denounce the armistice within forty-eight hours.

Of all the victors of the war, Italy was the most cruelly used: the victor without laurels, and without spoils—or almost; the victor who, it seemed, might have lost more than it gained. Armistice came to Italy on November 4, 1918, when the battle (or, more properly, the campaign) of Vittorio Veneto, which had begun on October 24, was finally won. With the help of the Allies, principally the British and the Americans, the Italians were able to drive the Austrians and a few German units back past the frontier.

"Peal of bells, clangor of military bands, flying of flags, choruses of people: This is what is adequate to the indescribable events of these days," wrote Benito Mussolini, who also celebrated: "This greatest joy is accorded to us: that of seeing an Empire annihilated, the violator of ours and others' freedom. . . . This is the great hour! . . . The hour of divine merriment, when the tumult of emotion suspends heartbeats and tightens the throat. The long passion, at last crowned by triumph, draws tears of joy even from eyes that saw much and wept much. . . ."

Only on the Italian front, as the Allies drove the enemy troops deep into Austria, was the territory of the Central Powers actually invaded. There it was patently evident that the Germans and the Austrians had been overwhelmed on the field of battle. With good cause the bells pealed everywhere, in all the countless churches of Italy, in the cities and the villages, in the valleys and on the mountains. Everywhere people were singing, and everywhere the red-green-white tricolor was flown. As in celebrations elsewhere, there were those who mourned because the victory could not bring back Italy's 600,000 dead, nor heal the blind and the maimed.

But even as the war ended, great political developments were taking place in Italy, too. And in Italy failure again, dogged the Socialists. As with most of Europe, the end of the war brought a sharp swing to the left. The time was ripe for a revolution that would oust the King and the aristocracy and set the stage for a

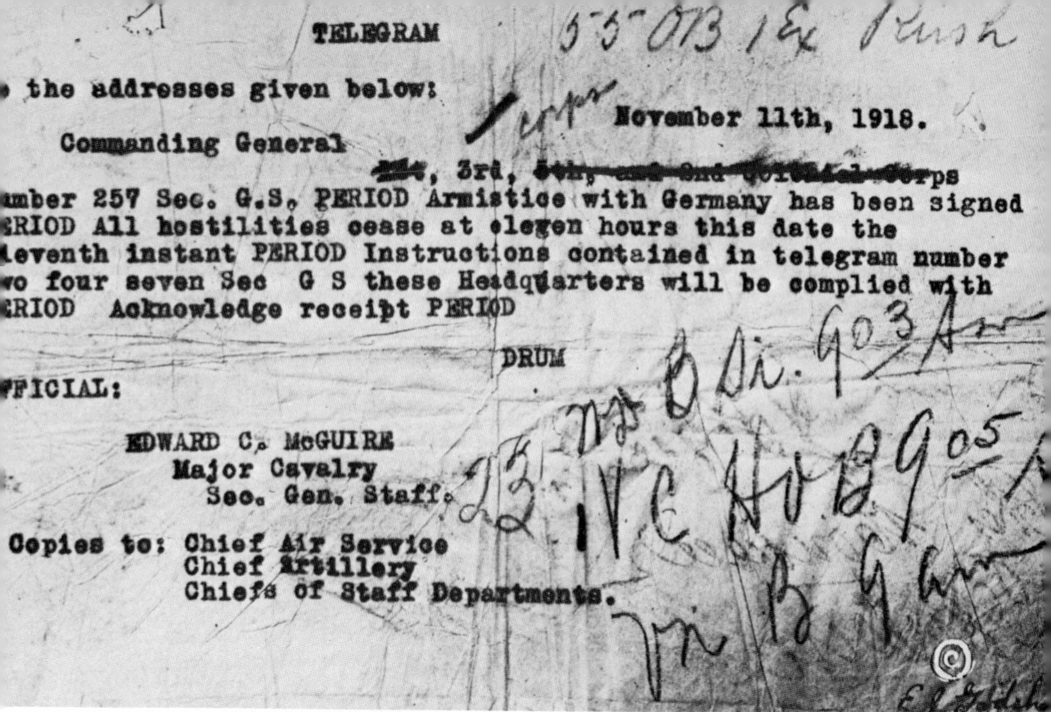

TELEGRAM

the addresses given below:

November 11th, 1918.

Commanding General

~~1st~~, 3rd, ~~4th, and 2nd Colonial~~ Corps

umber 257 Sec. G.S. PERIOD Armistice with Germany has been signed
ERIOD All hostilities cease at eleven hours this date the
leventh instant PERIOD Instructions contained in telegram number
wo four seven Sec G S these Headquarters will be complied with
ERIOD Acknowledge receipt PERIOD

DRUM

FFICIAL:

EDWARD C. McGUIRE
Major Cavalry
Sec. Gen. Staff.

Copies to: Chief Air Service
Chief Artillery
Chiefs of Staff Departments.

This telegram from Brigadier General Hugh A. Drum to Commanding Generals of Staff departments contains order for hostilities to cease. UNITED PRESS INTERNATIONAL

At the front, soldiers gave vent to unrestrained joy on being told of the armistice. UNITED PRESS INTERNATIONAL

In France, as in all Allied nations, cheering throngs crowded streets and other public places to hail the war's end.

THE BETTMANN ARCHIVE

In New York City the armistice brought a monumental snarl of traffic and an avalanche of scrap paper to Wall Street.

THE BETTMANN ARCHIVE

The armistice was greeted with dancing and merriment almost everywhere, as in this scene in the plaza surrounding City Hall in New York City. THE BETTMANN ARCHIVE

The Vanquished: Chief architects of Germany's military strategy General Paul von Hindenburg (left) and General Erich von Ludendorff confer with Kaiser Wilhelm (center) during the war. Later the Kaiser would be forced to abdicate. UNITED PRESS INTERNATIONAL

The Winning Team: General John J. Pershing, Commander American Expeditionary Forces; France's Marshal Ferdinand Foch, Supreme Allied Commander; Field Marshal Sir Douglas Haig.

UNITED PRESS INTERNATIONAL

This railroad car at Rethondes in which terms of the armistice were arranged has been preserved as a French national shrine.

UNITED PRESS INTERNATIONAL

Lone soldier guards a trench at a battleground near the Somme River in France, after the armistice. The troops have departed for embarkation points or the villages and cities. UNITED PRESS INTERNATIONAL

Parades, like this in Washington, were staged across America as the grateful nation welcomed returning troops after the war. UNITED PRESS INTERNATIONAL

Peace Conference: The big four who dominated the Paris Peace Conference in the Palace of Versailles were Vittorio Orlando, the Italian Prime Minister, British Prime Minister David Lloyd George, French Premier Georges Clemenceau, and United States President Woodrow Wilson. UNITED PRESS INTERNATIONAL

Before terms of peace could be arranged, war's apocalyptic companions, pestilence and famine, would claim more lives. The world-wide "Spanish" influenza epidemic caused some strange precautions against infection to be taken:

A California court session is held out-of-doors.

UNITED PRESS INTERNATIONAL

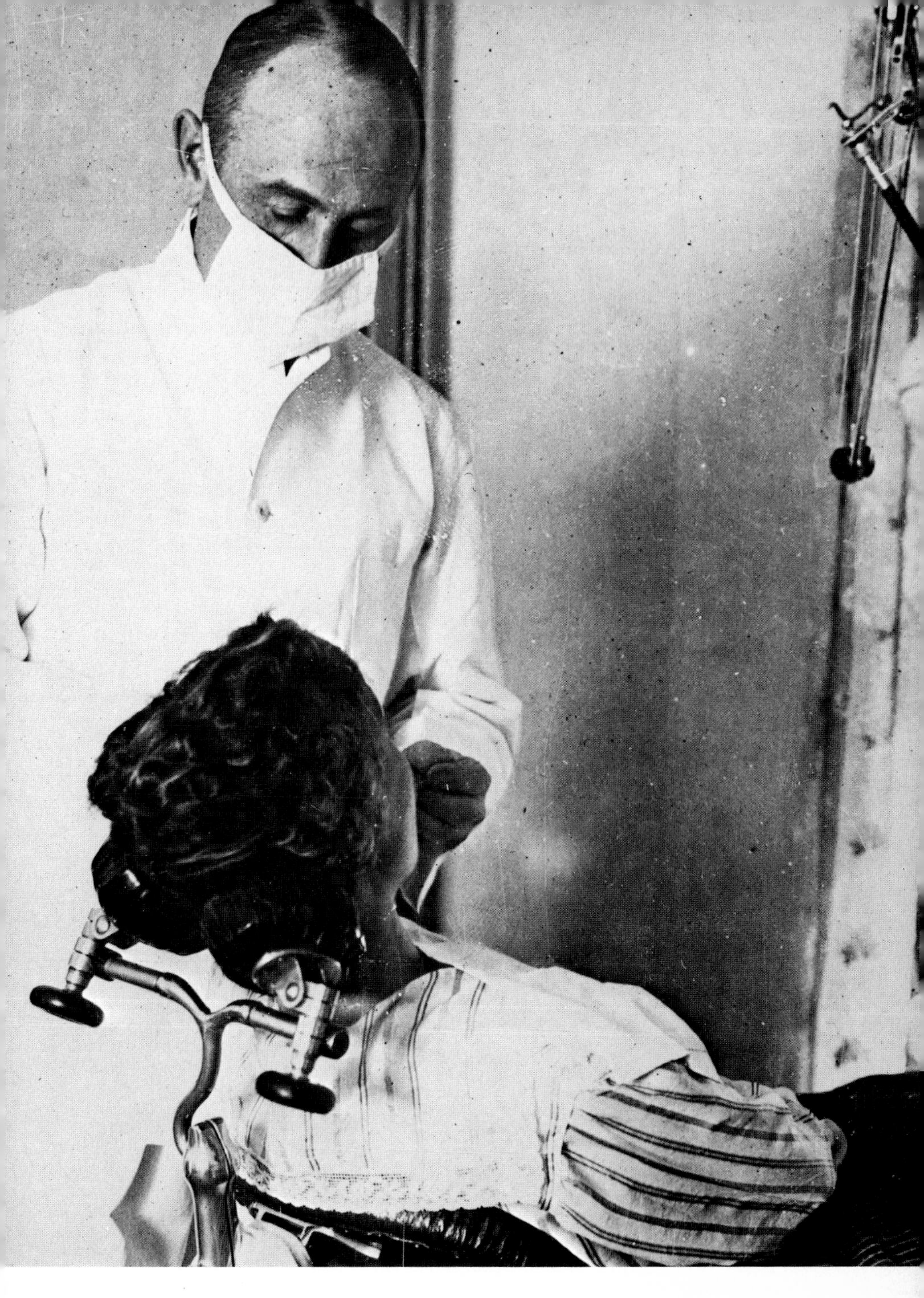

A wary dentist uses a gauze mask. UNITED PRESS INTERNATIONAL

World tranquility was delayed further by social unrest that triggered the Russian Revolution of 1917. This is a demonstration in Moscow.

UNITED PRESS INTERNATIONAL

Nicolai Lenin, dominant figure of the Russian Revolution and founding father of the Union of Soviet Socialist Republics, is seen here with Joseph Stalin (left) who, after Lenin's death in 1924, became for almost three decades the most powerful leader in Russia.

UNITED PRESS INTERNATIONAL

After a brief career in foreign affairs for the Bolsheviks, Leon Trotsky (center) assumed the task of building the Red Army, members of which are seen in this photograph. (The loser in a power struggle with Stalin, Trotsky eventually left the country and took up residence in Mexico where he was assassinated in 1940.)

UNITED PRESS INTERNATIONAL

In the days following the armistice, Germany, too, was rocked by revolution. This is a revolutionary mass meeting in Berlin.

UNITED PRESS INTERNATIONAL

Postwar disgruntlement in Italy led to the emergence of Mussolini and the *Arditi* (Black Shirts). Here in one of his famous marches to Rome, Mussolini (left, with ribbon across chest) and his followers are cheered in Naples. UNITED PRESS INTERNATIONAL

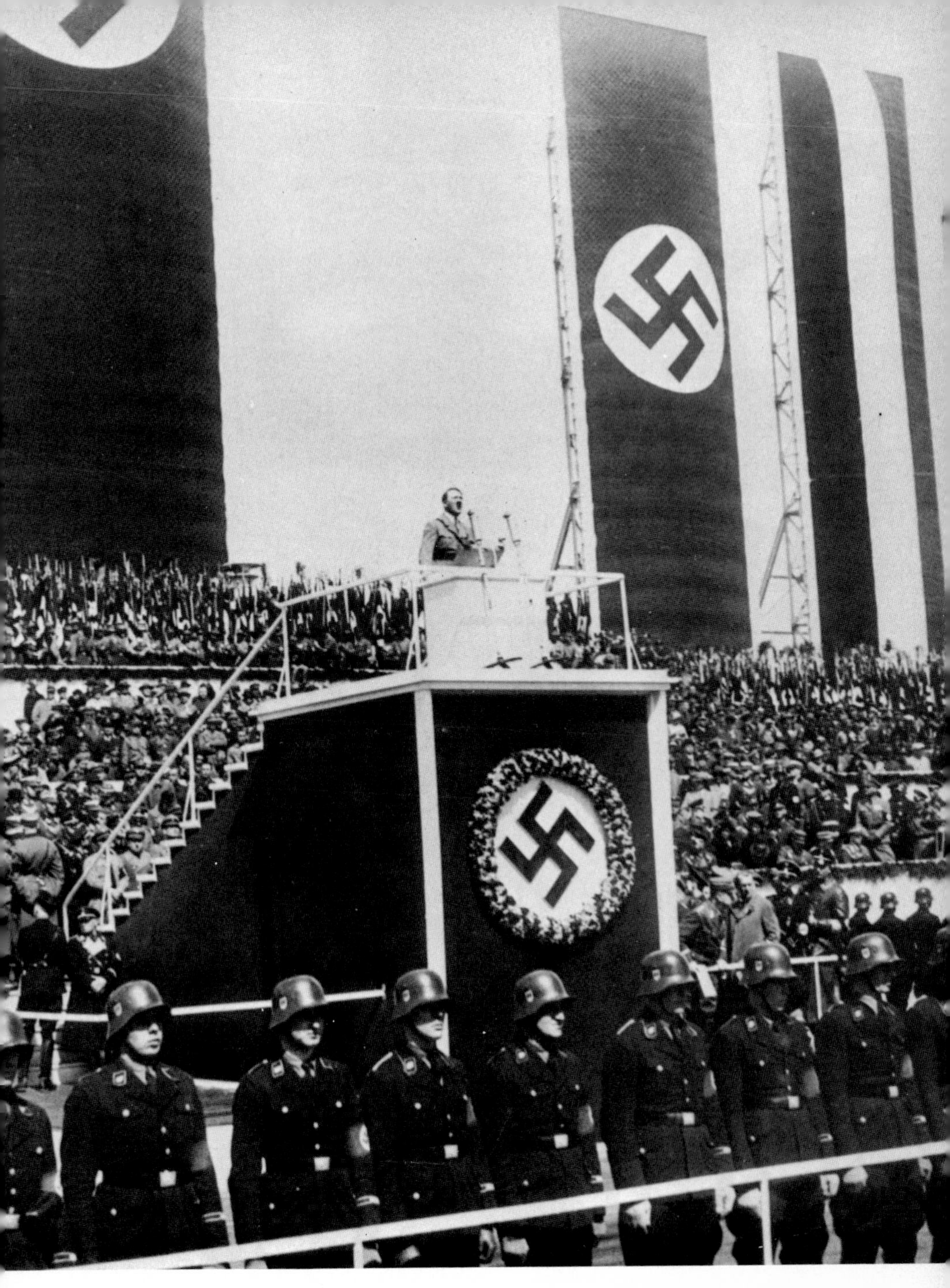

In Germany, the shaky political structure of the Weimar Republic would ultimately fall before the might of Adolf Hitler and his Nazis. Here Hitler is seen in a typical setting addressing a May Day gathering at Berlin's Tempelhof Airdrome. More than one million persons were reported to have assembled on this occasion.

UNITED PRESS INTERNATIONAL

*Il Duce* and *Der Fuehrer:* Mussolini and Hitler, postwar dictators of Italy and Germany, are shown during ceremonies marking a state visit by Mussolini. Their names would be inextricably linked to the history of the next generation. UNITED PRESS INTERNATIONAL socialist takeover. But the Socialists hesitated. They did not push for elections immediately following the armistice, even though elections almost certainly would have put their party in power, because of that fatal weakness of Socialists—intraparty quarrels. The right-wing Socialists argued that they did not want to "absolve the classes who willed the war from the terrible responsibilities of its results." This argument resembled the theory of the left-wing Socialists that nothing should be attempted "within the framework of capitalism," since the bourgeoisie was doomed, and it was better to let it collapse under the weight of its own mistakes and impotence. As time went on, the left-wing Socialists became more and more interested in copying the Bolsheviks in Russia, and at this juncture the schism among Socialists developed. Said Angelo Tasca:

> The fundamental weakness of Italian socialism was due to its lack of true revolutionary spirit. . . . The Italian Socialists waited for the middle class to die off naturally, without considering whether its death struggle, as they assumed it to be, if unduly prolonged, might not generate seeds of decay which would infect the whole nation, the socialist movement included. They behaved like the sole heir to an estate who prefers not to turn up till the last minute, just before the will is read. While they waited they confined their activities to "separating their own responsibilities from those of the ruling classes." This separation was, up to a point, justified and even necessary. But responsibility for evil committed is always shared by those who have failed to prevent it; and we have no right to connive at others' actions unless we are prepared to step in at the right moment and succeed where they have failed.

At that time it was the policy of the Italian Communists—as with Communists elsewhere—to hold back and let things get as bad as possible. This is a policy with a lot of built-in risks, since it depends too much on factors that may change and it may too easily alienate—for lack of action and accomplishment—the mass of the people on whom it must rely for the base of its power.

Precisely that happened to the whole leftist movement in Italy, socialist and communist alike.

Part of the problem was that the Italian leftist leaders, no more than the diplomats at Paris, realized the changes that had taken place in this country. Young men—and young women—by the hundreds of thousands had been uprooted from their villages and farms and spent four years in either the military or the factory. And now they were back, filled with the unrest that overtakes the human spirit after a long period of travail—and they found little in Italy to assuage that unease.

For even beyond the fact that jobs were hard to find, because of the widespread unemployment sweeping across Italy, there was little understanding of the feeling of this whole generation that had shared a common experience of an uncommon nature. The whole mass of ex-servicemen wanted a new life; they had vague, half-formed ideas that led them to seek contact with each other and to seek to strive for their common salvation. There was the disillusion with the war and a real feeling that "we must not be taken in again." The socialist leaders might have channeled this ferment to their parties' ends but they did not, and circumstances were not ever again so favorable to them.

By the Treaty of London of April 26, 1915, Italy agreed to go to war within the month against Austria. The terms of the treaty included the promise of territory for Italy—the ethnically Italian Trentino, the Austrian South Tyrol, and the predominantly Slavic Dalmatia. Also pledged to Italy was a part of the possible territorial acquisitions from Turkey and an "equitable" share of German colonies. (No provision was made to give Italy the Italian city of Fiume, which under the Austro-Hungarian monarchy had enjoyed the privilege of a free port.) Italy declared war on Austria May 24, 1915. At the end of August 1915 Mussolini was drafted; his military career ended in 1917 because of wounds he received during howitzer practice.

At first a consensus prevailed among the Allies that the war should be fought to a finish and internal political dissension forgotten until victory was achieved, but disenchantment with that policy set in when Italian intervention failed to turn the tide for the Allies. Orlando began to draw criticism for allowing "radicals" so much freedom—like Socialist Claudio Treves, who in July 1917 told the Chamber of Deputies that "next winter not another man will be in the trenches." There was even further disillusionment with Wilson's Fourteen Points, which led Gabriele D'Annunzio to write an article entitled "Victory of Ours, You Shall Not Be Mutilated!" a super-patriotic polemic typical of D'Annunzio, in which he complained that the Allies were lopping off the limbs (or territories) due to Italy as part of the spoils of war. For a time the Italian Government encouraged such outbursts of patriotism, for they bolstered Italian territorial claims at the peace conference. Yet, while the Italian representatives at the conference were taking their uncompromising stand over Fiume and Dalmatia (which irritated an already irritable Wilson and hardened him in his position), they lost their chance of gaining any of the German spoils in Africa.

On April 24, 1919, Prime Minister Orlando and his delegation returned to Rome in a boycott of the peace conference; two months later his government was forced to resign and Francesco Nitti took over. On September 12, 1919, D'Annunzio occupied Fiume to the consternation of Nitti. The following June, Nitti, too, would resign. The forces were gathering which would lead to Victor Emmanuel III's invitation to Mussolini to form a cabinet, to serve as prime minister, to march on Rome on October 30, 1922.

Perhaps Italy's most significant celebration of the armistice had taken place in Milan, for both Mussolini and the Arditi were there. (The Arditi, or Black Flames [literally, "the darers"], were the cream of the army's special assault troops. They had chosen for themselves a special all-black uniform. Even their flags were black. Because of the reckless violence of the Arditi, who staged street brawls on the slightest provocation, they became an embarrassment to the authorities, and there was considerable public demand that they be demobilized.)

On November 10, Mussolini had been one of several speakers at an armistice celebration held at the Obelisk, memorial to the Milanese heroes of the Risorgimento, and after the ceremony was over Mussolini walked over to a waiting truck, filled with Arditi;

the truck drove off through the streets to one of Milan's biggest and most fashionable cafés.

As Germany's nazism is said to have been formed in a beer hall, so Italy's fascism may be said to have been born in a café. The champagne flowed freely, and Mussolini offered a toast:

> *Arditi!* Fellow soldiers! I defended you when the Philistine was defaming you. I feel some of myself in you, and perhaps you recognize yourselves in me. You represent the admirable, warlike youth of Italy. The flash of your knives and the roar of your grenades will wreak justice on all the wretches who want to hinder the advance of the greater Italy! You shall defend her! We shall defend her together! Black flames, . . . to whom the honor? To you!

The next day the Arditi came to Mussolini's office and presented him with one of their flags—black, with a white skull on it—which he hung on the wall behind his desk. Like Hitler, he now had his cadre of bully boys.

The road that would ultimately lead Mussolini to power was already becoming clear to those who heard his speeches. Early in 1918, Mussolini, speaking in Rome following the Italian defeat at Caporetto, took to task those persons in high places—including the Pope, Benedict XV—who opposed the war as a "useless massacre." Such sentiments Mussolini regarded as being almost equal to the military reasons underlying the defeat. He recommended arrest and punishment for those who opposed the war for:

> Whoever has been to the front and lived in the trenches, knows what an effect the reading of certain speeches and Parliamentary reports had upon the minds of the soldiers. The poor man in the trenches asked himself: "Why must I suffer and die, if they are still discussing at Rome whether there ought to be war, if those who are at the head of affairs there do not know whether or not it is a good thing to be fighting?" That is deplorable and criminal talk, gentlemen! And now, even after Caporetto, after defeat, irresponsible people are allowed to make public antiwar demonstrations.

> The game is such that we must go on, because there is no other solution than this; victory or death! And it is the life or death of the nation that is at stake. . . . There is no turning back; we must win! . . . No! Italy will not die, because Italy is immortal!

The speech is important because as well as anything else, it captured the nationalistic spirit abroad in Italy; and Mussolini, the upstart editor, becomes joined via oratorical ardor with D'Annunzio, poet and almost legendary hero.

At war's end, his socialist pacifism behind him, Mussolini could declare that the war "was imposed by historical necessity" and had vindicated Italy's ideals and goals in that the Italian flag now flew "from the Brenner to Trieste and Fiume." Too, "the most magnificent political panorama which history records" was unfolding, as empires, kingdoms, and autocracies appeared to "crumble like castles built with cards." In this new day, Dante's lament,

> *Ahi! serva Italia, di dolore ostello,*
> *Nave senze nocchiero in gran tempesta.*
> Alas, slave Italy, the home of all griefs,
> A ship without a rudder in a great storm,

no longer need apply because according to the future *Duce*:

> . . . Italy today is no longer a slave; she is the mistress of herself and her future. She is no longer a rudderless ship in a storm, because a glorious horizon has been opened up by her victory.
>
> And the people are the rudder of this ship, which, between three seas and three continents, sails serenely and securely toward the port of supreme justice in the light of the redeemed humanity of tomorrow.

Mussolini's rhetorical optimism notwithstanding, Italy at the close of the war had a good deal of the rudderless ship about her. Her upward of 600,000 killed and two million wounded (half a million disabled) added up to a proportionately greater blow than the other Allies suffered, and she, of all the Allies, had the greatest problems of demobilization. Unlike England and France, Italy had no vast prewar industrial system into which to absorb the war-displaced working people. Moreover, the roads of immigration were closing. Whereas almost nine million people had immigrated into the United States from Europe in the decade 1901–1910 (in one year, 1913, Italy alone had sent nearly one million across the Atlantic), in the decade 1921–1930, the number would be more than halved, to just over four million.

Further, compared to France—or even Germany—and certainly England whose great empire was still intact, Italy had no natural resources to support an industrial complex that would come anywhere near supporting her nonagricultural workers. The war itself had, in fact, given the first real impetus to Italy's heavy industry. Italy had neither coal nor iron nor oil nor textiles. Wine, olive oil, food, and opera, yes; but no jobs.

Italy also differed from the other Allies in the reasons for waging war. To most Italians, the concept of Italy as a power—or for that matter a nation—was something of a novelty. Therefore, despite contradictory oratory, there had been no great "national ideal" to support the sacrifices of the war. The government's "sacred egoism," according to Tasca, had been "fundamentally neither egoistic nor sacred. Begun and carried on like a civil war, the war left a legacy of violent passions and insatiable hates. The day of victory brought no relaxation, and the defeats of 1916 and 1917 were only sparsely and belatedly avenged by the victory of Piave."

The depth of this trouble had not yet sunk into the nation's consciousness. In a time of triumphant joy now that the war was over and won, how could the future be anything save glowing? "The war had so turned and sifted the soil of existence, created such landslides and outcrops," Tasca concluded, "that it was felt that at the end of this geological epoch the sun would rise on a new world." Such millennial expectations were not peculiar to Italy or the common man. Had not Lloyd George also announced that "the postwar world is to be a new world. . . . After the war the workers must be inexorable in their demands." Even the pronouncements of the Italian Government interpreted the war as having ushered in a portentous age. "This war," proclaimed Orlando on November 20, 1918, "is also the greatest politico-social revolution recorded by history, surpassing even the French Revolution." These words were very fine while the war was on and for a very brief time after, but it soon became apparent that specific actions and major programs would have to support the talk before Italy would become a healthy nation.

Almost the first to feel the emptiness of life at home were the ex-soldiers who lived in the villages and the cities rather than on the farms. Shortly after the armistice groups of ex-soldiers from around the country, having met in a hit-or-miss fashion, banded together into the National Association of Ex-Servicemen. "No party, no class, no vested interest, no paper, enjoys our confidence," the association proclaimed. "Organized and independent, we formulate our own policy." In January 1919 the central committee of the association called for the formation of an ex-servicemen's political party. The first meeting took place in June. From the start it was apparent that the veterans found no common bonds with the Fascists, whose movement had then been under way for several months. The program the veterans approved looked the very model of democratic action. It called for the establishment of a Constituent Assembly; the abolition of the Senate, to be superseded by councils elected by popular vote; the reduction of compulsory service to three months; the proclamation of a fatherland "free from national egoisms and at one with humanity," etc. The program, as a member Emilio Lussu remarked, seemed "specially designed for collaboration with the Socialist party." It did seem that the ex-servicemen admired socialist ideals, especially their pacifism, and the socialist concern for the workingman.

One would have thought that this was the golden opportunity for the Italian Socialist party. Everything was in its favor, it seemed to have no opposition. And almost everybody in Italy, including the Fascists, were parroting socialist slogans and watching the party's every move.

But the Socialists did nothing. Two developments seemed to inhibit them. The first was political—Italy's treatment at the peace conference; the second was economic, at home. Mussolini's course of what has been described as "discontented nationalism" would eventually prove to be the effective one.

One is surprised by the memory that for a while Benito Mussolini had been one of Italy's leading Socialists. Mussolini was born in the village of Predappio. After a rootless young manhood (he had been a draft dodger in Switzerland and in prison as a radical), Mussolini earned the approval of party leaders in 1912 when he called for the ouster of those party officials who had supported the Italian war of conquest in Libya. In recognition of his efforts, the party made him director of the official socialist paper, *Avanti.*

Despite Mussolini's pacifist position in 1912, by October 1914 it was evident that the editor of *Avanti* was wavering between neutrality and intervention. Soon after that Mussolini made his decision and resigned his post at *Avanti*. On November 15 he published the first number of the *Popolo d'Italia,* which he subtitled "A Socialist Daily." On November 24 he was expelled from the Socialist party for his interventionist sympathies.

Italians of all political leanings were united in opposition to the indifferent treatment the nation received at Versailles. True, the government committed major tactical blunders in arranging for Italian officials in Dalmatia to send off hundreds of telegrams demanding annexation "in the name of the population"; in allowing government officials to make inflammatory speeches, reported in the papers, of course, pledging to defend Italy's rights to the death; and in permitting street demonstrations demanding the annexation of Fiume. None of this had the effect it was designed to have in Paris and, in fact, it only made things more difficult for Orlando and Nitti. And the entire Italian delegation spent so much time and effort on the Fiume question that it might as well not have been at the peace treaty conference at all. It came to the point that the conference was being conducted without the Italians. While the Italians argued, Fiume, Wilson, Clemenceau, and Lloyd George went about the business of the treaty. As Tasca commented:

> So, when Orlando and Baron Sidney Sonnino [his associate] decided on April 23 to leave Paris as a protest, their gesture

> fell flat, for it did not affect the situation. But Italian national feeling was stirred, and Orlando made fiery speeches to cheering crowds at railway stations. Parliament approved the action of the government, and Italy lived again in the atmosphere of maggio radioso [golden radiance]. D'Annunzio, Mussolini, and the nationalists demanded that the government should immediately annex Fiume, Dalmatia, the Tyrol, and present the Paris Conference with the fait accompli.

"We must put a fait accompli before the three powers," Mussolini wrote.

> The fait accompli is a decree of annexation to which the Jugo-Slavs, though they gnash their teeth, will have to submit. They cannot make war on Italy. They have no artillery, machine guns, aeroplanes, or munitions. They will go no further than a more or less vigorous diplomatic protest. It would be calamitous for the government to miss such a unique opportunity. If the question is not settled at once in accordance with the simple requirements of necessity, it will never be settled.

Italian feeling ran so high that there was talk of an actual alliance with the Hungarians, the Bulgars, and the Turks. The government tried to maintain the fiction that its gesture of walking out of the conference had been successful; and newspapers reported "the void created at the conference by the absence of Italy," the peace conference's "disorganization," and the "confusion" resulting from the departure of the Italian delegates, which overthrew the "Wilsonian dictatorship."

The peace conference, meanwhile, was working its way through its agenda—down to the question of the boundaries of Austria. Orlando and Sonnino could play their game no longer. Without delay they left for Paris. The boundaries of Austria were the boundaries of Italy.

For Orlando ("le tigre végétarien," Clemenceau called him) the trip back to Paris was one of disappointment and almost humiliation. Most Italians felt as if they had been cast aside after having borne their share of the fighting and the suffering, while the three major allies divided up the spoils of victory. This feeling of injustice was to be exploited to the hilt by Mussolini, and was one of the major factors in the appeal of fascism. It was to the advantage of the Fascists to have the Italians believe that they had been betrayed by their own allies, for later it would provide the emotional justification for Mussolini's military adventures abroad and for his defiance of the League of Nations. (When a Socialist, Mussolini had hailed the league as the hope of mankind.)

It has been argued indeed, that if the rulers of Italy had kept their heads in the years after the war and had not yielded to the threats of Mussolini and the Fascists, Italy might have taken the place of Germany and the Hapsburgs as the arbiter of Balkan politics. But while the other allies were sharing among themselves the German colonies in Africa and the former Turkish empire in the Near East, all of Italy's leaders were driving themselves into a frenzy over a few rocks in the Adriatic.

Those were part of the economic and political developments that made a great role for Italy impossible; the only recourse her politicians would find would be to use their diplomatic defeat as the excuse for a course of action that was to reduce Italy to a fifth-rate power.

So, as the Paris talks progressed, Mussolini was forging his Fascist party out of a rag-tail collection of disgruntled ex-army officers, pseudo-university students (whose families paid the costs of one course a year to keep them away from home), small shopkeepers resentful of taxation, and déclassés of every sort who wanted but nothing to destroy the existing order. All of these were the elements that gave fascism its early emotional aura of romanticism. And its fatal charm extended to industrialists and merchants and bankers and manufacturers as well, and thus gained a base of financial support. The *Popolo d'Italia* (Mussolini's paper) contended that the state was incapable of providing public services and that they should be handed over to private industry (comparable to proposals in the United States that private enterprise take over the post office department). There was, indeed, a meeting held in Genoa in April 1919, at which many of Italy's leading industrialists and landowners adopted a program to set up a private industrial combine to take over the state monopolies that had been set up during the war—a move that Mussolini was only too eager to back. Tasca comments on "the ideological duality which was one of Mussolini's chief assets [and which] enabled him to satisfy both the value passions of the mob and the more precise interests of the capitalists."

In addition, following a meeting of the Fascisti, at about the same time, Mussolini drew up a statement that forecast Italy's disdain of the League of Nations:

> The Congress declares its opposition to the imperialism of other peoples at the expense of Italy, and to the contingent imperialism of Italy at the expense of other peoples. It accepts the chief principle of the League of Nations, which presupposes the integrity of each nation; integrity which, so far as Italy is concerned, must be realized in the Alps and the Adriatic through her claim for Fiume and Dalmatia. We have a population of forty millions in an area of 287,000 square kilometers, cut across by the Apennines, which reduce still further the cultivable land at our disposal. Within from six to twenty years we shall be sixty millions, and we have only a million and a half square kilometers of colonies, of which the greater part is desert and quite unsuitable for settling our excess population. But if we look around we find England, with a population of forty-seven millions and a colonial empire of fifty-five million square kilometers; and France, with a population of thirty-eight millions, had an empire of fifteen million square kilometers. And I have figures to prove that every nation in the world has a colonial empire, which it is far from ready to give up for the sake of transatlantic creeds. Lloyd George speaks openly of the British Empire. Imperialism is the basis of life for any nation seeking economic and spiritual expansion. We say that either everyone must become an idealist, or no one. Let us seek our own interests. We want our place in the world, because we have a right to it. Let us be frank; the League must not

become a trap set by the wealthy for the proletarian nations as a means of perpetuating the present conditions of the world balance of power.

Appealing to the disaffected of Italy and the rich, to the Catholics and the anti-clericists, to the monarchists and the republicans, to the Socialists and the anti-Socialists, Mussolini was now mapping out the road of Italy's future.

In the end what was to give him power was his program of action, which was especially attractive to the eighteen-to-thirty-year-olds of Italy. Fascism showed them the easiest way to the glory road. Everything was simple, there were no such things as doubts or uncertainties, no conflicts or second thoughts. The young Fascist in a world he did not know existed could joyfully affirm: "I need not think; therefore I am."

At the same time, in another peninsular state, Spain, a congeries of military, religious, political, and intellectual ferments was bubbling under the rule of Alphonso XIII. Ever since the defeat of the Armada, Spain seemed to have been a victim of history; her defeat in the war of 1898 had been only the last in a series of losses at home and abroad that contributed to Spain's gradual decline in standing among the powers of the world. (In addition, it left Spain's army—or her military caste—with nothing much to do except to meddle in politics and to drain off resources from the national economy that might very well have been better used in solving the nation's industrial problems.)

The years between 1898 and 1918 saw Spain torn by all manner of problems. In Morocco, Spaniards and particularly Spanish workers on the railroads were continually being harassed by Rif tribesmen; this led to calling up the reserves, which in turn led to bloody riots in Barcelona. Barcelona and Saragossa were the scene of other riots due to industrial upheavals: Socialists, anarchists, and syndicalists all found fertile grounds among the factory workers of Spain to sow the seeds of revolt. The two main political parties, the Liberals and the Conservatives, were suffering a weakness of leadership, with the result that almost none of the reforms that either party wanted to institute were ever carried through.

And, of course, the all-important church in Spain was forever engaged in the battles to insure its own preeminence, battles within the state itself and with the mother church at Rome.

When World War I broke out, Spain was almost equally divided in her sympathies. The intellectuals and the nonextremist trade union leaders were on the side of the Allies; the church, the army, the bureaucracy, and the upper classes were on the side of the Germans. It was perhaps just as well, in view of this, that Spain remained neutral.

It was during this war in which she did not fight, oddly enough, that Spain's generals were able to achieve one of their great triumphs, for it was in 1916 that the Army began to organize its secret "juntas de defensa," allegedly to promote military efficiency; but before long the rulings of the juntas were being used in an attempt to run the government. The supreme triumph of the military came in June of 1917, when a whiff of revolution touched Spain and a group of senators and deputies were inspired to set up a series of commissions to report on reforms that should be undertaken. Before the commissions could act, the Socialist General Workers Union launched a general strike aimed at establishing a socialist republic—a strike the army briskly ended with machine guns, leaving the juntas the only real power in the country.

And all this time, the man who was to be the ultimate beneficiary of the power of the juntas was far away from Spain. Francisco Franco Bahamonde, born at El Ferrol in 1892, entered the military academy at Toledo in 1907, and in 1910 volunteered for service in Morocco. There he spent the years of World War I; he would not come to fame until 1936, after the civil war had already broken out, when he would organize the transport of troops from Spanish Morocco back to the mainland to take part in the fighting.

It was through no plotting of Franco's that Spain was to become the testing ground for World War II.

# V

# THE EAST TAKES LEAVE OF TRADITION

A reform is a correction
of abuses; a revolution
is a transfer of power.
BULWER-LYTTON

WESTERN AND RUSSIAN AUTHORS from John Reed to Boris Pasternak to George Kennan have described the Russian Revolution as one of the shakiest enterprises ever undertaken by man. The storming of the Winter Palace, said the American historian John Lukacs, was "something out of a comic opera or a very old movie."

Even to the men involved in it—until they later fell victim to the very human desire to make events more heroic than they actually were—the events of November 7, 1917, were confused and seemed of negligible importance. A few squads of Bolshevik soldiers moved into some government buildings and the czarist government's counterattack was weak, disorganized, and ultimately futile.

The cruiser *Aurora,* which had been captured by the Soviets, steamed along the Neva; for hours it did not fire at all, and when it did, it fired blanks.

In *The History of the Russian Revolution,* Trotsky wrote: "It was the most popular mass-insurrection in all history. The workers had no public need to come out into the public square in order to fuse together: they were already politically and morally one single whole without that."

But Trotsky was being romantic. The city of Petrograd hardly knew what was going on; the normal life of the city was barely disturbed. Thousands of bicycles and trolley cars carried the workers to and from their usual jobs, and at the very moment that the Winter Palace was being "stormed," Feodor Chaliapin was singing *Don Carlos* at the opera. The troops at the Winter Palace, including some riflewomen, were the kind of troops held at the home front in time of war: either too young or too old for combat, ill-trained and inexperienced. The Palace itself was a rabbit-warren of a place with endless doorways and entries, so that it seemed that instead of being attacked it was being explored by small clusters of armed Bolsheviks who ran up and down the stairs and along the corridors, occasionally firing a gun. But there was more shouting and arguing than there was gunfire, and there was very little bloodshed. That was to come later, under the Communists. The Bolsheviks, though they did not know it, had set off one of the great revolutions in history with all the epic heroism of a family quarrel.

Whatever the defects of the revolution, the revolutionists faced a major problem immediately. Their first aim was to get out of the war, but their plans were to be snagged. The Bolsheviks had believed that their revolution, once started, would sweep all of Europe—at least, certainly, Germany. Not only had Bolshevik orators, over and over again, promised the people of Russia a peace "without annexations or indemnities," they had gone so far as to promise that they would never make peace with the Kaiser, but only with the revolutionary government that would certainly take over Germany.

Events overtook oratory. In the hope that the Germans would catch the spirit of revolution, the Bolsheviks encouraged "fraternization" among the troops in the trenches, but the German Army on the Eastern Front was as tough as ever and showed no signs of defalcating. Nor were Great Britain or France in any mood to talk peace. With the entry of the United States into the conflict, they were now assured of victory. The Bolsheviks had more than their promises driving them to make peace: there was the steadily deteriorating military situation. In equipment and armaments the army of the Czar had never been the equal of the Kaiser's, and Russia lacked adequate industrial and transportation systems to support her armies. Partly because equipment and armaments were in an atrocious condition, her casualties approximated Germany's. (Germany suffered 1.8 million dead, 4.3 million wounded, and 620,000 taken prisoner; Russia 1.7 million dead, 5 million wounded, and 2.5 million taken prisoner.)

Russia's situation was made even more critical by the fact that once the revolution was established, the peasants deserted the armies in hordes in order to get back to the estates on which they had been serfs so that they could get their share of the expropriation.

"They voted for peace with their feet," said Lenin with some acerbity.

Still, Lenin was the Russian leader who argued that to save this foundling state, a peace must be signed with Germany as quickly as possible, even though the German demands included the annexation of Poland, the Baltic states, and much of the Ukraine. If the Germans crushed Russia, the revolution would fail, for Russia was the only state where Communists held power. With peace, revolutionary Russia could be organized, and with time, the fight for world communism, the revolution of the proletariat, could be renewed.

Lenin's argument that it was necessary to ask peace of the Kaiser's government, rather than run the risk of having the revolution extinguished, had hard sledding. Nikolai Ivanovich Bukharin, who had left the editorship of the revolutionary newspaper *Novy Mir* (*New World*) in New York to join the revolution, headed the party of the "Left Communists," the war party that insisted on continuing the "revolutionary war against imperialism." Bukharin argued that if Russia left the war, the Kaiser would be all the more able to contain any revolt in Germany; that the revolution would disgrace itself if it betrayed German and international socialism to save its own skin; that even if the Soviets were defeated in battle, it would be preferable to existing in shame and disgrace. (Bukharin had a flair for being on the wrong side in Soviet dialectics. Although he allied himself with Stalin during the latter's rise to power in the twenties, he opposed Stalin's policies of forced industrialization and agricultural collectivization and was stripped of his positions in 1929; among other things he had been editor of *Pravda*. In 1938 he was tried for treason and was executed.)

In the midst of all this, Trotsky tried to offer a middle course. (He was in charge of the delegation at the peace talks at Brest-Litovsk.) On the one hand he agreed with Lenin that Russia was incapable of continuing the war, but on the other hand he agreed with Bukharin that the revolution would be disgraced if it accepted the peace terms laid down by Germany. One of his hopes at Brest-Litovsk was to drag out the negotiations long enough so that the communist revolution could catch fire in Germany, and to this end his speeches before the German and Austrian delegations, rather than dealing with the matters at hand, were long and inflammatory tirades against the German Government, aimed at inspiring the uprising of the German worker. Trotsky also succeeded in persuading the Central Committee of the Soviets to reverse its vote in favor of continuing the war to adopt a formula "neither of war nor peace." This policy was, of course, unfeasible, as events were soon to show.

Stalin, the realist, saw this. He was entirely unmoved by the oratory of the Left Communists and by their preachings of revolutionary morality; to him the notion of Russia's revolution sacrificing itself for the sake of the European revolution was simply ridiculous.

"In accepting the slogan of revolutionary war we play into the hands of imperialism," he said. "Trotsky's attitude is no attitude at all. There is no revolutionary movement in the West, there are no facts [indicating the existence] of a revolutionary movement; there is only a potentiality, and in our work we cannot base ourselves on a mere potentiality. If the Germans begin to advance this will strengthen the counterrevolution in this country. . . . In October we talked about a holy war against imperialism because we were told that the one word 'peace' would raise a revolution in the West. This has not been borne out. . . ."

But time and events were not to allow the Communists forever to argue what was to be done. As the arguments went on, the armistice broke down and the German armies advanced almost to Petrograd. The Ukrainian assembly signed a separate peace, and what there was of a Red Army was in almost complete rout. Finally the Central Committee accepted the terms of the peace, and on March 3 the treaty was signed. While Lenin had led the fight to accept peace, he still could—and did—denounce the treaty. As it turned out, however, by the end of the year the German and Austrian armies had been beaten, and the German Army was evacuating the Ukraine. The peace of Brest-Litovsk was academic.

The negotiations did have one enduring consequence, however.

From them Lenin emerged as the man to lead the party and the nation. He had shown an undogmatic logic and courage of conviction which enabled him to defy the party's prevailing mood, and an extraordinary power of persuasion which had enabled him to sway the mind of the party. The party and the country which had seen and heard him but little during the actual upheaval in October could now gauge his real stature, the real virtues of his mind and character.

Trotsky, on the other hand, suffered a temporary eclipse after the negotiations. He had exposed his major weakness—a lack of realism, a propensity for dialecticism and theatrical gestures in situations which called for neither. His eclipse was not yet serious; as far as the party was concerned his authority was still second only to Lenin's. He resigned from the Commissariat of Foreign Affairs to become Commissar of War, and in this new post he became the founder and builder of the Red Army. Among some party leaders his actions during the Brest-Litovsk crisis would be held against him several years later, in the bitter struggle over the successor to Lenin.

As for Stalin, he was already following his policy of remaining in the background as much as possible till the right time came, but he had made himself almost indispensable to Lenin in his fight against the "knights of the romantic phrase" and "ultra-revolutionary dreamers." And even this early, the differences between Stalin and Trotsky were beginning to emerge.

Lenin, Stalin, and Trotsky were presumably coequal, yet Lenin and Trotsky were far better known than Stalin—so much so that the government was generally referred to as the Lenin-Trotsky government. Lenin, older than Stalin, had an international reputation as a revolutionist and as a theoretician of the communist revolution, and Trotsky, almost exactly the same age as Stalin, had become almost the equal of Lenin through his brilliance as an orator and polemicist. Stalin, on the other hand, remained virtually unknown to the people at large. This was unbearable, commented biographer Isaac Deutscher, for a man who for all his extraordinary career "had never since his youth been able to still his yearning for distinction, the man whose nagging sense of inferiority had been perversely stirred even by his promotions."

For several years, Stalin was able to conceal his bitter hatred of Trotsky, but occasionally his temper would get the better of him and he would refer to Trotsky as "the grandiloquent poseur" and "the champion with the fake muscles."

What would really shape Russian history, even to the present day, was the fact that Lenin, and later Stalin, were tough professional revolutionaries, and once, almost by a miracle, the revolution had gained power, neither ever had any intention of losing it. But Lenin had to contend on all sides with the possibilities of total disaster: the war itself, the possibility of couterrevolution, collapse of the economy, and the chaos in that part of the world—all of Central and Eastern Europe.

The chaos got worse every day. The Allies, by now alarmed by the Bolshevik's seizure of power and the treaty which resulted in a one-front war for Germany, were giving all the help they could to the so-called independence movements of Central and Eastern Europe, most of which were anti-Russian as well as anti-German.

Against this background, Lenin looked around for the sort of men who would be able to help him with tough and decisive action in the crises to come.

The man he was going to rely upon more and more was Stalin, even though it seemed that the most difficult task of the new regime had fallen upon Trotsky: the building of the Red Army, upon which, above all else, the life of the new state would depend. As it has been said, when Trotsky set out to found the Red Army, he "seemed to be burning all that he had worshiped and worshiping all that he had burned."

For years the Bolsheviks had been decrying the military establishment of the Czars, and, indeed, of all the ruling powers—for obvious reasons—and they had relentlessly preached to the common soldier the gospel of revolt against the officer class. But now the shoe was on the other foot. Like every government, the Bolsheviks realized that to govern, they would have to have an army, and to have an army rather than a rabble they, like the Czars before them, would have to be able to enforce discipline. To come out and say this, of course, would be ruinous. The facts, in this case, would not sound like facts; they would sound like imperialist cynicism and what was worse like "betrayal of the revolution."

For two sermons that the Bolsheviks had preached were now coming back to haunt them. One was that once the revolution had been won there would be no wars at all; peace would prevail and there would be no need for armies. The second was that even if a small army were needed it should be a thoroughly democratic army in which the common soldier should have the right to elect his officers, and there should be soldiers' committees to make sure that the rights of the common soldiers were not disregarded.

Trotsky was hardly in a position to explain at length in public what he had no hesitance in saying privately, that soldiers' committees might be all very well and good in training camps but they were of no use at all on the battlefield. So he skirted the issue entirely, and he made his first appeal not to the soldiers as a whole but to the members of the party. Here his argument was that he needed their help, that only with their help could the revolution succeed. The revolution had been successful in its first great task, he said, destroying the old order; now it faced the necessity of building the new order on those ruins. The rule of the day was to be "work, discipline, and order." Shortly after Trotsky's establishment of the Red Army—an army as disciplined as he could make it, in contrast to the theoretical ideal of the people's militia—came the establishment of the Cheka (a name made up from the initial letters of the Russian name for Extraordinary Commission to Combat Counterrevolution and Sabotage). Here was the secret police of the Czar, or now of the state, back with a vengeance, just as with the army.

At first the Cheka had only minor powers—the ability to take away food rationing cards, for example. Soon, as the severity of "incidents" began to increase, and fired by Lenin's frequent public calls for the "shooting of speculators and counterrevolutionaries on the spot," stories of Chekists pulling out their guns and shooting up restaurants and cafés where they heard criticism of the regime began to increase. (One famous shooting incident occurred in a circus, where Bim Bom, a well-known clown of the day, was making jokes about the regime. Cheka gunfire struck four of the audience. The Cheka admitted later that it might have been better to wait until after the performance to arrest Bim Bom.)

The revolution became the property of the Bolsheviks because they understood the uses of power. While the anarchists and the Socialist Revolutionaries clung stubbornly to slogans and their promises, the Bolsheviks were willing to compromise dogma, according to the realities of a given situation.

Lenin once said that "the question of power is the fundamental question of every revolution," and the Bolsheviks seemed fascinated by the uses of power; sometimes it seemed that their responses were inspired by the sole desire to see what the reaction would be. In fact, what may be Stalin's most famous comment—"How many divisions has the Pope?"—indicates at once Russian cynicism and naïvete concerning the nonmilitary factors at work in western politics.

To the Bolsheviks, what had been means became ends; what they had sought to destroy was now their sole objective: power, its control and its possession. The party of the revolution became the party of dictatorship. (Idealists in the West continued to believe in the methods of the revolution long after the makers of the revolution had abandoned them, but that is always the difference between the believers and the doers.) As Lenin said when he was accused of betraying the world revolution: "Yes, we shall see the international world revolution; but for the time being it is a . . . fairy tale—I quite understand children liking beautiful fairy tales. But I ask: Is it seemly for a serious revolutionary to believe in fairy tales?"

And so the methods of the revolution began to change almost from the start. One of the first projects the Communists had to back away from was their concept of agriculture. The first step in agriculture, according to the Communists, would be the transformation of "each private estate into a sufficiently large model farm to be conducted, at the expense of the community, by the local Soviet of agricultural workers under the direction of trained agriculturists, with the use of the best technical appliances."

A vision of Utopia as particular as this could come only from a city-bred revolutionist, since it totally disregarded what has been called the fourth instinct, described by Robert Ardrey in *The Territorial Imperative* as the instinct of ownership. The peasants of Russia, given all the promises they had heard, did not propose to trade the landlord of the aristocracy for the landlord of the proletariat. They wanted ownership of the land and reluctantly—but trading land for space, as they had done at the treaty of Brest-Litovsk—the Bolsheviks went along. Thus one of the first acts of the communist regime was simply to set up a new class of landed proprietors.

A slightly different problem arose with the communist takeover of industry where Lenin frankly admitted that the aim of the revolution was simply to take over the institutions of capitalism.

> Capitalism [he said] has simplified the functions of [management] and has reduced them to such comparatively simple processes as to be within the reach of any literate person. . . . As for the organizational form of the work, we do not invent it, we take it ready-made from capitalism: banks, industries, the best factories, experimental stations, technical schools. . . . We need only adopt the best models furnished by the experience of the most advanced countries. . . . The most important thing is to instill into the oppressed and laboring masses confidence in their own power.

In a short time, Lenin found that it was far easier to expropriate industry than to manage it, and that the average worker could be just as slovenly and lazy under communism as he had ever been under the Czars.

> Our work of organizing the proletarian worker has obviously lagged behind the work of expropriation. The art of administration is not an art that one is born to, it is acquired by experience. Without the guidance of specialists in the various fields of knowledge, technology, and experience, the transition to socialism will be impossible. Because of the indispensability of the specialists we have had to resort to the old bourgeois method and to agree to pay a very high price for the services of the best bourgeois specialists. Clearly such a measure is a compromise, a departure from the principles of the Paris Commune, a step backward on the part of our socialist Soviet state power, which from the very outset pro-

> claimed and pursued the policy of reducing high salaries to the level of the wages of the average worker. The sooner we workers and peasants learn to acquire the most efficient labor discipline and the most modern techniques of labor, using the bourgeois specialists for this purpose, the sooner we shall liberate ourselves from having to pay any tribute to these specialists.

Another step was to follow soon; Lenin was now having to institute "discipline" on the proletariat itself. "Large-scale industry," he said, "calls for absolute and strict unity of will, which directs the joint labors of hundreds, thousands, and tens of thousands of people. Today the revolution demands, in the interest of socialism, that the masses unquestionably obey the single will of the leaders of the labor process." Later, Lenin was to observe:

> We had counted on being able to organize the state production and the state distribution of products on communist lines in a small-peasant country by order of the proletarian state. Experience has proved that we were wrong. It transpires that a number of transitional stages are necessary—state capitalism and socialism—in order to *prepare* by many years of effort for the transition to communism. . . . We must first set to work in this small-peasant country to build solid little gangways to socialism by way of state capitalism. Otherwise we shall never get to communism; we shall never bring these scores of millions of people to communism. That is what experience, what the objective course of the revolution, has taught us.

It was all these factors—the increasing pressures of the regime on the workers and the peasants, the ruthless suppression of the anarchists and the Socialist Revolutionaries—that contributed to the increasing bitterness of the civil war.

Because the war was so bitter and so fractured and because the unifying force of the royal family and the nobility had been taken away, it seemed for months that a single country could never again be forged out of Russia. What was being fought was not one big civil war, with clearly defined battlefronts, territories, and separate armies, but a whole series of small wars with varying sets of antagonists. There was, of course, the Red Army against the South Russian Imperial (White) Army. The latter in the summer of 1919 came within a hair of victory. During the same period, whole groups of peoples struggled to be freed, not only from the Bolsheviks but from Russia as well: Ukrainians, Georgians, Armenians in the Caucasus, the Don and Kuban Cossacks.

Another element that contributed to the bitterness of the fighting was that the leaders in Moscow, convinced of the need of cracking down in order to keep control of the country instituted extremely repressive measures. The peoples of Russia had at first welcomed Bolshevik rule because Lenin and his associates had promised every group and every nationality freedom and equality. But before the revolution was even completed, the peasants were being ordered to turn food over to the state; Trotsky was establishing a discipline in the army the likes of which no Czarist Chief of Staff would ever have dreamed of trying to introduce; and the Bolshevik drive to revive industrial production by setting up work standards prompted a workers' delegation to tell Lenin, "One sees that you, too, Comrade Lenin, take the side of capitalists."

Now workers and peasants, realizing that the slogan of the dictatorship of the proletariat was a slogan and nothing more, that what the revolution was doing was to trade one set of repressive rules for another, began to rebel against the very leaders they had welcomed only a few months before. They had fought for Soviet rule, which in those days meant rule by a local council picked by themselves, and had expected to solve the problems of the local community (or factory or regiment) with a minimum of interference from Moscow. But the year 1918 was to see the end of that dream. Down from Moscow to the towns and villages came the communist commissars (more often than not accompanied by a member of the Cheka) to dissolve the local Soviets on the grounds that the members were members of the bourgeoisie who must be replaced by genuine Communists, chosen by the Commissar. In the rebellions that went on and on, well into 1921, it is surprising now to see how often the slogan of the uprising was:

"Long live the Soviets; down with the commissars." To many an old Russian still living today, those were the golden days, those brief months when the real Soviets ruled, before the Communists destroyed them.

The great advantage of the Communists was that even among those western powers that understood what was happening (Churchill thought that Bolshevism would become a major threat to Europe unless it was throttled in its infancy), the war against the Central Powers so completely engaged their forces that they were without any ability to intervene. At one time, there were twenty-odd governments threatening the Moscow regime, but they remained only threats. In addition, as military historians point out, the Communists held the center of the country; the White forces, on the periphery, became less effective the more territory they conquered. Also, despite the many uprisings, to many of the peasants and workers, the White Russian forces represented the return of the old landlords and masters, and, often, the White Russians took their revenge in a fashion that justified the peasants' fears.

Finally, the anticommunist forces failed because they could not work together; for this the first blame falls on the military forces loyal to the Czar, though considering the working of the military mind, which reveres authority above all, their failure is comprehensible. To them, the real rulers of Russia were the aristocrats who had already fled. Ironically, therefore, whenever the White Army conquered a territory and established a civilian government, it would consist of those very people whom the army considered guilty of having deposed the only true government. Most of the governments in White Russian territory represented a strange spectrum of political thinking from the ultra-conservative to the radical left. The breakdown of such a jerry-built political structure as this was only a question of time.

Meanwhile, the Bolsheviks consolidated their rule. Against the ramshackle anticommunist local governments, torn with suspicion and given to oratory, the Bolsheviks used swift and decisive action. (This as much as anything else eventually brought many of the Czar's soldiers into the Red Army. They deserted the White Army's cause in contempt of squabbling politicians and joined

Trotsky's army when they saw him turn to discipline, competence, and professionalism.) Too, despite facts to the contrary, a majority of Russians still believed in such revolutionary slogans as the doctrine of "national self-determination." Even though the communist use of the phrase, "the people's republic" of such-and-such was soon shown to mean nothing except paper independence, the words continued to have great propaganda appeal. Lenin must be given a great measure of credit for making somewhat credible the Bolshevik promises that separate nationalities within Russia have autonomous existence.

Lenin never took his eyes off his main goals: consolidation of what the revolution had gained, then the broadening of the revolution. He believed in waiting; he could shrug off the loss of Finland, of the Baltic states, of Poland, even of that part of Siberia held by Japanese occupation troops. After Admiral Alexander Kolchak was defeated in Siberia in the winter of 1919–20, Lenin warned the local Communists about "premature sovietization." He felt that it was wiser to have an "independent" Siberia for the time being, one that could be made part of Russia in the future. He warned his associates—and ordered his inferiors—against the danger of giving way to their passion for centralizing and sovietizing. Whatever his other shortcomings, Lenin had patience.

While the Russian state was undergoing its birth pains—and in the space of only fifty years was to become one of the dominant powers of the earth—another giant was undergoing a period of vast upheaval. The first years of the century had seen the first great political changes in China: the fall of the Manchus, the Boxer Rebellion, the turn of China from the west to Russia. The last development seems today to Americans the most tragic development, for the West had an ironic store of goodwill in China at the end of the nineteenth century. It had accrued from the speed and ease with which Japan had defeated the corrupt and incompetent military forces of the Manchus in the brief Sino-Japanese war of 1894, and the subsequent widespread belief in China that the Japanese victory was largely due to the "westernization" of Japan.

During the summer of 1898, Emperor Kuang Hsü issued one

edict after another, drafted by his advisers and aimed at the modernization of China: the civil service was to be reformed; new schools teaching western subjects were to be introduced; a reformed army based on universal conscription was to be established; departments of agriculture, trade, and the arts were to be formed. But to the tragedy of China, these reforms raised such a furore that the most ferocious of all dowager empresses, Tzu Hsi (the emperor's aunt and regent during his minority), emerged from her retirement to head a palace revolution. Kuang Hsü, virtually a prisoner in his own palace, was reduced to the status of puppet while the Dowager Empress ruled once more as regent. The Empress rounded up as many of the Emperor's reform-minded advisers as she could find, executed them, and revoked their edicts. In addition, to stifle any remnants of reform thinking, the Empress embarked on a savage campaign to rid China of all foreigners. Then would follow the bloody Boxer Rebellion in which scores of missionaries and other foreigners, thousands of Chinese Christians, and the German minister were murdered.

In 1908, both the Empress and the Emperor died. This left the throne to an infant two and a half years old and the government to a powerless regent. The dynasty was toppled by the revolution of October 1911 during which China was declared a republic. The first national assembly elected Dr. Sun Yat-sen to serve as Provisional President. However, Dr. Sun—the son of a tenant farmer, a convert to Christianity and a political visionary whose opposition to the Manchu dynasty had caused him to be exiled—lacked the special administrative skills required to at once, mend the schisms that divided China's peoples and to resist the aggressive designs of Japan and Russia upon her territory.

Sun Yat-sen soon resigned his Presidency to Yüan Shih-k'ai, who seemed more likely to be able to unite the country, and in the four years following 1912, Yüan seemed to be on the road to success.

Two things were to defeat him: the rise of the warlords in the provinces and the coming of World War I.

The warlords were the perpetual throwback to the dark ages for China. They took over the provinces to pillage, they lived by rapine and murder. They set the stage for the development of the final Chinese Revolution by destroying all the strengths of order in the country. Their depredations, for example, caused most of the landowners to flee the country and take refuge in the cities, leaving behind their agents to collect the rents. The agents soon found that the only way to operate—much less to make their own fortunes—was to form an alliance with the warlords. And thus the peasants were alienated from any form of government save that of force and threat.

At this time, too, civil government in the provinces was reduced to impotency because none of its plans or its orders had any force against the guns of the warlords. Those men in the local governments who had any pretensions to learning or to improvement fled to the universities, leaving the provinces to the incompetent. The rise of destructiveness, besides all its human and social consequences, very soon was to have its economic results. Neither the warlords nor the bandits with which China became infested nor the landlords had any intention of putting capital into the improvement and maintenance projects that the agriculture of China demanded; the great irrigation and flood control systems that had been standard features of the countryside for generations began to fall into disrepair. Roadways and river facilities began to disintegrate, railroads and telegraph lines broke down. In short, the country was slowly disintegrating, and with it—though it was not generally recognized then—the prestige of the West. The West's brief period of great prestige in China was now vanishing.

It may be true that western democracy, as a political concept, never had a fair chance in China, but all the average Chinese knew was that in the time when the political institutions of the West had been in charge, corruption continued unchanged and unchecked, the warlords and the bandits continued to rule the countryside, the economy was steadily declining, oppression and poverty had never been worse. As C. P. Fitzgerald observed in *The Birth of Communist China:*

> The Chinese are not romantic, particularly in politics. No lost cause appeals to the Chinese, no fallen house receives

> sympathy or support. What has fallen is down and can never be raised up. There have been no restorations in China, no Jacobites, no ghosts from the political past. . . . The mass of the people neither regretted the Empire, nor hoped for its return. They probably expected a new dynasty, they disliked what they saw of the Republic, yet in a vague way they felt that the Empire could no longer meet the need. Something was required which would suit Chinese ways and yet adapt itself to changed conditions. No one really thought that a new dynasty, encumbered by the memories of the past, would prove able to steer China on to a new course. By 1920 it was clear that western democracy was not the solution, and tacitly it was abandoned even by the revolutionary element.

If the problems posed by the warlords were long range (they were to hold de facto command of the country until the mid-twenties), the advent of World War I proposed more immediate problems for China. For one thing, interests were always shifting among the foreign powers bent on the exploitation of China. While as recently as 1913 Yüan was able to negotiate a loan from a consortium representing the financial interests of Great Britain, France, Russia, Germany, and Japan, the moment that the world war broke out, Japan saw an excellent opportunity to oust one of her great trading rivals, Germany, from the Chinese outlets. Disregarding the temporary Chinese neutrality, and Chinese protest, the Japanese took over German possessions in the province of Shantung. To complicate the problem, China herself was still split. On August 14, 1917, China finally did declare war on Germany, a move that brought decidedly mixed blessings.

It was obvious that China would make no substantive contribution to the war, torn as she was by her internal convulsions, and without resources of men, money, or munitions; and the question of whether to enter the war had led to the establishment, in effect, of two governments: one under the control of the military and headed by Tuan Ch'i-jui at Peking, plus a provisional Kuomintang (Nationalist) government at Canton, headed by Sun Yat-sen. The entry into the war, belated as it was, did lead to a seat at Versailles for China. The delegation there, which represented both Peking and Canton, made what might seem today a reasonable series of demands: that the Japanese-seized properties at Shantung be returned to her, that all foreign troops be withdrawn, that communication systems—post offices, telephones, and telegraphs—be returned to the Chinese, that the so-called spheres of influence agreements be canceled. None of this was granted. The peace conference ruled that all matters except the Japanese occupation of Shantung were internal affairs of the Chinese nation and therefore not subject to action by the conference; and then it ruled that Shantung belonged to Japan. Thus the western powers succeeded in turning even pro-western Chinese against them.

A good many Chinese intellectuals felt that Peking had been induced to declare war for the sole purpose of allowing the Allies to take possession of German ships that had taken refuge in her ports, and for taking over other German resources in China. Accorded "perfidious" treatment at Versailles, the Chinese refused to sign the peace treaty.

China did become a member of the League of Nations by signing the peace treaty with Austria, for that treaty did not contain the Shantung clause; and she signed a separate treaty with Germany that canceled both the indemnity she was to pay Germany for her share of the Boxer Rebellion damages, and Germany's extraterritorial rights in China. This was small repayment, however, in view of the other damages done China; and anti-western demonstrations, especially by students, were commonplace in Chinese cities in 1919.

But the next year seemed to bring about a total change in world thinking toward China. For one thing, the new revolutionary government of Russia had finally gained control of Manchuria and Siberia, previously held by the White Russians, and Russia had no desire to have the possibility of a conflict with China on her distant borders, so she approached China with a proposal to give up *her* extraterritorial rights and to negotiate a new agreement. At almost the same time, the United States called a Washington conference for the purpose of putting all future financial loans to China under international control, and so to prevent any individual nation from gaining further influence in China; preoccupied with the development of her own West and with the Philippines, the United States was about the only western power that did not have designs on China.

Three important developments came out of the Washington conference: foreign post offices were abolished in China as of January 1, 1923; the treaty limiting naval armaments, in effect, solidified Japan's domination of Asia's northeast coast, as the western Allies were to find out twenty years later; and the Japanese began to exhibit a much more friendly attitude to her giant neighbor. Though Japan held on to some mines and land holdings, other German possessions in Shantung were returned to China, and a conference was convened in Peking in 1926 for the purpose of discussing tariffs.

By that time, however, China seemed beyond hope as a functioning nation. Her government was virtually powerless. Ironically, ever since the end of the war, as her international position had improved, her internal governing power had disintegrated. In Peking, Hsü Shih-ch'ang and Tuan Ch'i-jui were in such control as there was, but in Canton the Kuomintang had Sun Yat-sen as President, and in Manchuria still another set of leaders (Wu P'ei-fu, Ts'ao K'un, and Chang Tso-lin) were vying for power. In 1922, Li Yüan-hung became President, and the capital was established in Peking.

"Hopes for a united China, however," commented one observer, "proved illusory. Funds were insufficient, cabinets unstable, Parliament venal, and in June 1923 Li Yüan-hung again fled the capital. In October 1923 the Parliament, probably as a result of heavy bribes, elected Ts'ao K'un to the Presidency and a 'permanent' constitution was promulgated."

Few enough in the western world realized what was happening in China in the 1920's: that the appeal of communism, slowly at first but then stronger and more strongly, was charming the minds of the Chinese leaders. Few western leaders have apparently ever comprehended that the western concept of democracy not only has no particular appeal but does not even have meaning for people outside the influence of the Greco-Roman, Judaic-Christian heritage. What western leaders wanted to see in China was the outward form of an orderly nation. Sun Yat-sen failed with the

West because he was regarded as a revolutionary—and ironically failed in China because he was not revolutionary enough; he did not grasp power and ruthlessly employ it.

Rebuffed by the West, Sun turned to Russia. Russia's envoy to Peking, Adolf Joffe, was ignored by the western embassies, but he was feted by the Chinese, and in particular by Sun. Thus the first tentative alliance was made between the Kuomintang and communism; the newborn Chinese Communist party, created almost simultaneously in China and in Paris in 1921, was provided with an atmosphere in which it would be able to grow. It is true that in the interim another powerful Chinese leader, Chiang Kai-shek, would be able to gain control of the country from the period starting in 1926, and that there would be a full-scale war with the Japanese that would merge into the Second World War before the Communist party would be able to take over in China, but the day would come.

Sun—as he himself described—felt an almost instinctive relationship with the Russian Revolution. Even before the First World War, he had met Russian revolutionaries in Europe and had found common bonds: Russia and China were both vast and backward nations—indeed, approaching the size of continents; both had been ruled for generations, even centuries, by dynasties long out of touch with the evolving world, bypassed by the Industrial Revolution, the economy basically agricultural, necessitating a large peasant class. It was almost inevitable that the new Kuomintang, unified after Sun Yat-sen's death in 1925 as it had never been during his life, dedicated as it was to the recovery of sovereign powers for China, should lean to communism for guidance. For Russia, ruled by communism, was the one foreign power besides the United States not attempting to make capital of China. While the western powers were preaching democracy in China, what they were practicing was imperialism. (Chiang Kai-shek, in his book *China's Destiny,* blamed most of China's problems on this imperialism.) In 1918, Sun had sent a message of congratulations to Lenin, urging him to continue on in the communist struggle, and inasmuch as it was about the only message of congratulations that Lenin received from another head of state, it was triply welcome. The "Light of the East," Lenin called the message. Sun, in fact, had long dreamed of two developments that the Russians were able to implement—the one-party state and an economic program that included expropriation of land and control of capital.

Virtually all the leaders who came on to vie for control of the country after the death of Sun belonged to the middle, or the upper middle class. Chiang, for example, was the son of a fairly prosperous business family well enough off to send him to military school in Tokyo—Chinese pragmatism at its most basic. The first revolution in 1911 sent him scurrying back to Shanghai to join the staff of General Ch'en Ch'i-mei, and through Ch'en he met Sun Yat-sen and Chang Ching-chiang, a wealthy and powerful broker. He also became acquainted with Huang Ching-yung, one of Shanghai's better-known underworld characters, and it is presumed that he became a member of the Green Circle, at this time the most powerful secret society in Shanghai. Chiang, in short, knew all sorts of people in the city who had access to power, or money, or both. After the military situation cooled off, Chiang became a stockbroker on the Shanghai exchange, where he got into money difficulties. Like many another broker, he had been able to make a fortune in the bull markets of the war, but when the war ended he did not foresee the crash and was caught short. He was bailed out of his money troubles by Chang Ching-chiang and his other rich sponsors and was sent off to Canton to help Sun Yat-sen.

The first leader of the Chinese Communist party was Ch'ên Tu-hsiu, an intellectual and a professor at Peking University. Among the first members was Mao Tse-tung, an assistant in the library at Peking. The Chinese students corps in Paris was also founding a branch of the party, and among them was Chou En-lai.

It may be significant that these men learned about communism only from books and talk; certainly none of them had done any real traveling in Russia. And none were workers or came from a working background. Leaving aside Ch'en, who was an intellectual, and Chou En-lai, son of an ancient mandarin family, there was Mao, the equivalent of a British feudal yeoman, the son of a farmer who had his own small land holdings. As pointed out many times, however, these leaders came from the provinces of

China where the influence of the West was the weakest but the most hated, where the landlords were the most oppressive and the military the most vicious.

Mao in those days was passing through a part of his life that he later thought, as all men are prone to do, was both the bitterest and the best part. Mao was young, twenty-four, and very poor and in love. Peking then was like the St. Petersburg of the 1870's—rich, sleepy, dusty, untroubled by what was happening in the world. At the university, Ch'ên Tu-hsiu's first editorial for his magazine *New Youth* had said: "The task of the new generation is to fight Confucianism to the death. All the old traditions of virtue and ritual, all the old philosophies, all the old political subtleties and the old learning, all must go together. We must break down ancient prejudices and build a new society based on democracy and science."

Mao had come to Peking with a number of theories in mind. He had been graduated from the Teachers' Training College in the summer of 1918. At Peking he wanted to study languages, particularly French and English. (He had once wanted to write a history of the French and American revolutions.) Also, he would be able to support himself by taking care of students who, even at that hot spot in world history, were off to France under a so-called work-and-learn program that the French had instituted to at once help solve their war-made manpower-shortage problems and to keep what friendly ties they had with the Chinese. Mao helped organize the students, steered them through a French-run orientation program, and saw them off on the boat.

Once the students were gone, however, Mao was alone in Peking (as far as friends were concerned), without a job and with a great desire to become an intellectual. What he had to guard against, what was to worry him most, was that Peking then as now, and like many of the ancient university-capitals, was filled with students who were driven largely by desperation. They were smart, these students—as they still are today—and even brilliant, but their society had no use for them. No place, no jobs. Mao was more fortunate than most. Through friends he was able to meet Li-Ta-chao, librarian of Peking University, later to become founder of the Chinese Communist party. Mao was given a job in the library—getting newspapers for the students and putting them back when they were through. It was a menial position, and Mao got little more money than the coolies and the sweepers. But what burned into his soul was that the students poring over the newspapers he brought them treated him as though he were not there, and if he got up the courage to ask a professor a question, he was simply not answered. Years later Mao would recall how much he learned to hate the students and professors he met at the University of Peking. "I knew then," he said, "that there was something wrong. For hundreds of years the scholars had moved away from the people, and I began to dream of a time when the scholars would have to teach the coolies, for surely the coolies deserve teaching as much as the rest."

But there was a better side of life for him. He had fallen in love with Yang K'ai-hui, the daughter of his philosophy professor, and, as can happen, it seemed to give him greater self-confidence. Through the endless snows of the Peking winter, he worked in the library of the university from seven in the morning to nine at night, walked the city, and was in love. He married a year later.

Where the Dowager Empress had sought by the knife and the ax to hold China in the nineteenth century—or preferably get it back to the fourteenth—Japan had lunged forward into the twentieth. Mutsuhito, or Meiji Tenno (*Tenno* being Emperor and *Meiji* meaning "Enlighted Peace," the name he adopted for his reign), was crowned Emperor in 1868. The country's power structure was still divided over the merits of the 1854 treaty with Commodore Perry that had opened some Japanese ports to foreign trade. In Japan, unlike China, some of the most powerful feudal lords (the *daimios* of Satsuma and chōshū, for example) opted for opening the country up. When Meiji Tenno moved the capital of the country from Kyoto to the city, renaming Tokyo (formerly Yedo), and took an oath to institute a number of reforms including an assembly, he again was supported by a majority of the daimios.

By giving up their estates and most of their privileges to the Emperor, the feudal lords effectively put an end to the special rights that had been the foundation of feudalism. A whole new program of western-style modernism was introduced. The European calendar was introduced; foreign languages, including English, were taught in the schools; the first railroad, between Tokyo and Yokohama, was constructed; and a legal system based on the Napoleonic Code was introduced.

Indeed, the development of Japan in the fifty years between 1875 and 1925 was as astonishing as the development of Russia that was to follow. Economically, politically, and militarily, Japan had made herself a world power in those years. She had also developed a near-fatal flaw—the overwhelming influence of the military. This influence first became evident in 1918, when Japan was among the powers who sent troops into Siberia to fight the Bolsheviks. In a way this action was the prelude to the later confrontation of the Japanese and the Chinese. The Japanese General Staff, which very much modeled itself on that of the Germans, took control of the Siberian operation out of the hands of the civilian leaders. For the purpose of giving them experience, it committed far more troops than necessary and continued action long after the other powers had withdrawn.

This independent action by the army in defiance of the government gave rise to the so-called dual diplomacy that marks the conduct of foreign policy after the usurpation of power from civilian authorities by the army in the name of its right of autonomous command. (In almost every case such independent actions were recognized by the government after the fact, since not to do so was to admit both at home and abroad that the civil government was unable to control the military.) The Siberian expedition was followed by the invasion of Manchuria in 1931, and the rise of the military to total power was increasingly evident.

Japan's turn to militarism had more than one cause, of course. In the nineteenth century, Japan had been a small and somnolent nation ruled by an efficient dynasty. Her agrarian economy had been equally efficient—enough so that it was an exporter of foods. Then Japan plunged headfirst into the twentieth century and suddenly found itself victim of its new efficiencies. The first major problem was the explosion in population that followed the introduction of contemporary western techniques in medicine and hygiene. The nation became increasingly dependent on the rest of the world for food imports as well as for raw materials required by its growing industrial plant. For industry had supplanted agriculture at the base of the nation's economy.

Industrialization, however, had been paralleled by the growth of the concept of tenant farming as the backbone of the agricultural system, with the result that the standard of living of peasants (whether rural or urban) was enormously improved.

As the nation became increasingly modern and complex, an ever-widening gap developed between the city and the country, between the industrial worker and the farmer, between the educated elite and the common man. Moreover, the upper classes—the politicians, businessmen, intellectuals, and military leaders—all had different perceptions of the nation's destiny. Consequently this bursting, diversifying nation which within a generation had achieved true contemporaneity—modern modes and methods in education, finance, transportation, and politics—lacked strong and unified leadership. Therefore it was almost inevitable that the military move in when the vacuum of leadership developed. Since the best opportunity for advancement in any military establishment comes in time of war, it was only a question of time before the military establishment of Japan would force the nation into a war—and, in the end, into a war that could not be won.

One of the paradoxes of history is that the island monarchy of Japan, built on militarism and imperialism, should feel itself strong enough in 1941 to challenge the power of the western world—and lose; while another great island monarchy, built on socialism and imperialism—and among the challenged—would win. Still, within twenty years, Japan, a loser, would again be moving to the forefront among prosperous nations while Great Britain, a victor, would be among the debtors of the world.

Woodrow Wilson's Fourteen Points, however ephemeral they may have seemed to the realists of the West, had a different meaning for the idealists of the world. The Fourteen Points became a touchstone of polemic throughout the countries of Latin America, and in the United States, W. E. B. DuBois and Marcus Garvey—each in his own way laying foundations that now support the black power movement—saw Wilson's international fiat as part of a philosophical justification of their theses.

In India the Fourteen Points gave hope to such men as Gandhi, who had turned his back on his own deep conviction of pacifism to recruit soldiers for the British Army in the belief that the British would grant self-rule to India after the war if only India would help while the war was still going on. When Britain, the war won, turned to achieve mastery of India again, Gandhi began his twenty-eight-year struggle for independence.

In 1918 Mohandas Karamchand Gandhi was forty-nine years old. He had been born in Porbandar, a tiny princely state in the Kathiawar peninsula of western India. Both Gandhi's father and grandfather had served with distinction as Chief Minister of Porbandar. The family was cultured and well-to-do by Indian standards. This was true despite the fact that their social background was relatively plebian. The Gandhis belonged to the Vaisya caste, third highest of the four traditional Hindu castes.

Young Gandhi was physically weak, timid, and self-conscious. At the age of seven, he had been betrothed for the third time, two girls chosen for him earlier having died in turn. He was married at the age of thirteen to a girl named Kasturba, also thirteen. The marriage was to last sixty-two years.

Gandhi spent his formative years in an orthodox Hindu home and was educated in Indian schools. He completed his university studies in Bombay, then went to London to read for the bar at the Inner Temple. At this time his personality and his outlook had already been fashioned by his traditional Indian environment. Thus, his two years in London were but a passing phase. They provided him with a legal training but did not leave any lasting imprint on his character, thought-processes, or way of life. He returned to India in 1891 basically unchanged, entirely an Indian, in no sense an Englishman.

After a few years at the bar, Gandhi was invited to South Africa to plead a case on behalf of the Indian community against discriminatory legislation enacted by the Transvaal Government. He expected to remain a year but stayed on for almost twenty. It was there that he experimented successfully with his novel method of political action, satyagraha or nonviolent noncooperation, a technique which was later to revolutionize Indian politics and to galvanize millions into action against the British raj.

He returned to India in 1915, already a famous man. Receptions were held for him and honors were heaped upon him in recognition of his efforts on behalf of the Indians in South Africa. Gandhi was embarrassed by the praise he received and promised to make good the honors by serving the people of his homeland. Between 1915 and 1918 Gandhi attracted a number of followers in India, but despite his fame among the educated classes, Gandhi was not a well-known leader of the people. General popularity would not come until later, with his dramatic resistance to the repressive Rowlatt Bills, which gave the British sweeping powers of arrest and imprisonment over suspected political agitators.

In February of 1918 Gandhi helped to lead a strike on behalf of the textile workers in Ahmadabad. During the second half of 1917 plague had ravaged the area. In order to induce the workers to stay, the millowners had offered them a sizable bonus. When the plague was over, the employers withdrew the bonus.

The dispute was referred to a committee of arbitration. But before the committee could begin its work, the millowners declared a lockout on February 22. They opened the mills again on March 11, offering the weavers a 20 percent wage increase. The weavers demanded a 50 percent increase and refused to work. Gandhi, after investigating the situation, thought that 35 percent was a reasonable compromise and persuaded the workers to accept it. But the millowners remained adamant.

Gandhi now proceeded to launch a struggle on behalf of the workers. To lead the strike successfully, Gandhi laid down these conditions: never to resort to violence; never to depend on alms; to remain firm, no matter how long the strike continued; and to earn bread, during the strike, by any other honest labor. The laborers pledged themselves at a general meeting not to return to the textile mills until either their terms were accepted or the millowners agreed to refer the dispute to arbitration. Under the shade of a tree on the bank of the Sabarmati, Gandhi held daily meetings and issued leaflets. The workers, who attended the meetings in thousands, were reminded of their pledge and of their duty to maintain peace and self-respect. Daily the workers paraded the streets of Ahmadabad in peaceful processions, carrying their banner bearing the inscriptions *El Tek,* "keep the pledge."

The strike situation began to grow critical. During the first weeks, the workers showed courage and self-restraint and staged massive daily rallies, but as time went by, they began to show signs of weakening. Gandhi would not allow the weavers to degrade themselves by begging, but to provide the work needed for sustenance by thousands of people was not easy. Gandhi now feared that the lack of progress would lead to rioting and almost certain loss of the struggle. Attendance at the daily rallies began to dwindle, and the look of defeat appeared on the faces of those who did attend.

Gandhi was still trying to achieve a settlement when, as he later said, an idea occurred to him at a workers' meeting. "Let us both starve," he said, "in trying to keep your vows. Unless you rally and continue the strike till a settlement is reached or till they leave the mills altogether, I will not touch any food."

The strikers were not prepared for this. One of them got up and said: "Not you, but we shall fast. It would be monstrous if you were to fast. We will now remain faithful to our pledge to the end."

"There is no need for you to fast," said Gandhi. "It is enough that you could remain true. As for me, I will break my fast only after the strike is settled."

A number of strikers shared the fast with Gandhi on the first day, but he dissuaded them from continuing it further. The fast electrified the textile workers and restored their morale; the millowners, too, since this was a new technique in labor relations, were dumbfounded. At the end of three days, the owners agreed to arbitration and Gandhi broke his fast. The employers celebrated the occasion by distributing sweets among the laborers, and a settlement was reached within a few days. At the settlement meeting, held under the very tree where the pledge had been taken, both the millowners and the government commissioner were present to celebrate the settlement. The commissioner advised the strikers: "You should always act as Mr. Gandhi advises you."

There was no breathing space for Gandhi. Hardly was the weavers' strike over, than he was off to attend the grievances of the peasants in the Kheda district; there, too, he advised recourse to satyagraha, and after four months of the nonviolent struggle, the peasants' pleas were substantially granted.

All this time he was also making speeches on behalf of a number of other causes: for the emancipation of women; for the return to native dress; for the use of the native tongues of India, particularly Hindi.

It should be remembered that in 1918 Gandhi was only one of a half dozen or so nationalist leaders. Like them, his goal was freedom for India; but unlike some of them, he was willing to achieve this goal within the British Empire. He looked forward to commonwealth status for India, rather than complete independence. And like most other leaders, Gandhi felt that this goal would be achieved by India's enthusiastic participation in the Allied war effort.

At the War Conference at Delhi in April 1918, the Viceroy had requested Gandhi to support the resolution on recruiting. Gandhi did, in a single brief sentence which he spoke in Hindustani: "With a full sense of my responsibility, I beg to support the resolution." His words had infinitely more effect because of the language he used; it was the first time in living memory that anyone had spoken in Hindustani at a viceregal meeting.

In his letter to the Viceroy which he wrote afterward, Gandhi explained why he supported the recruitment resolution:

> I recognize that in the hour of its danger we must give, as we have decided to give, ungrudging and unequivocal support to the Empire of which we aspire in the near future to be partners in the same sense as the Dominions overseas. But it is the simple truth that our response is due to the expectation that our goal will be reached all the more speedily. On that account, even as performance of duty automatically confers a corresponding right, people are entitled to believe that the imminent reforms alluded to in your speech will embody the main general principles of the Congress-League scheme, and I am sure that it is this faith which has enabled many members of the conference to tender to the government their full-hearted cooperation.
>
> If I could make my countrymen retrace their steps, I would

> make them withdraw all the Congress resolutions and not whisper "Home Rule" or "Responsible Government" during the duration of the war. I would make India offer all her able-bodied sons as a sacrifice to the Empire at its critical moment, and I know that India, by this very act, would become the most favored partner in the Emipre, and racial distinctions would become a thing of the past. But practically the whole of educated India has decided to take a less effective course, and it is no longer possible to say that the educated class does not exercise any influence on the masses. I have been coming into most intimate touch with the ryots [peasants] ever since my return from South Africa to India and I wish to assure you that the desire for Home Rule has widely penetrated them. I was present at the sessions of the last Congress, and I was a party to the resolution that full responsible government should be granted to British India within a period to be fixed definitely by a Parliamentary statute. I admit that it is a bold step to take, but I feel sure that nothing less than a definite vision of Home Rule to be realized in the shortest possible time will satisfy the Indian people. I know that there are many in India who consider no sacrifice too great in order to achieve that end, and they are informed enough to realize that they must be prepared to sacrifice themselves for the Empire in which they hope and desire to reach full status. It follows then that we can but accelerate our journey to the goal by silently and simply devoting ourselves heart and soul to the work of delivering the Empire from the threatening danger. It will be national suicide not to recognize this elementary truth. We must perceive that, if we serve to save the Empire, we have in that very act secured Home Rule!

Gandhi's work for British recruiting was ended when he became seriously ill, an illness made even more serious for his obstinate refusal of all medical aid; he would not take medicine, he would not eat, even the rather odd foods on which he then subsisted, such as peanut butter and lemons; he would not even drink fruit juice. Gandhi's friends finally insisted on calling in doctors.

"But what could they do," asked Gandhi in his autobiography, "with a patient who would not listen to them?" The doctors diagnosed a nervous breakdown. Gandhi was convinced that he was dying and began to devote all his waking hours to meditation and prayer. His body was slowly wasting away.

The second half of November Gandhi spent at Matheran, a hill-station. He took a slight turn for the better and in mid-December he went to Bombay for medical treatment. He was ordered to drink milk to rebuild his body, but he had long ago sworn never to drink milk. He experimented with sweetened water, almond and bean oil, as substitutes for milk, but he began to worsen again and became weaker and weaker. His wife argued with him that his vow referred only to cow's milk or buffalo's milk; he had had only these two animals in mind. She argued that it would not be against his vow if he drank goat's milk. By now, Gandhi had determined that he wanted to live, and he "somehow beguiled" himself, as he later put it, into agreeing with his wife on the interpretation of his vow, and allowed himself to be fed goat's milk. His health gradually began to improve.

India now was at a critical turning point, the basis for which can be found in the great expectations of self-determination that were unleashed during the war. As that terrible conflict drew to a close, the temper of both discontent and eager anticipation were increasingly evident throughout the entire nation; the principle of self-determination for all peoples that had been proclaimed by President Wilson had stirred the imagination of the Indian intelligentsia, and the hopes and aspirations of all classes had been raised by the British pledge of ultimate self-government for India, contained in the Montagu Declaration of 1917, a landmark in the history of the *raj*. The first installment of self-government had been promised for soon after the war; now the actual proposals of how it was to be achieved were being anxiously awaited. The period of preoccupation with the war was giving way to a new wave of political consciousness. As elsewhere throughout the entire world, the war had served as a violent catalyst for social and economic change such as no war before had ever produced: inflation and the shortage of consumer goods caused by a total war that sucked up all but the barest life essentials of economic production and led to widespread frustration and despair. And in India as in the rest of the world, the forced speedup of industry and commerce had strengthened the influence and aspirations of the Indian middle class, especially the businessmen. In addition, returning servicemen were beginning to demand equality of treatment and a better way of life. In the Punjab in northern India, revolutionary groups were actively challenging British authority. Then came the Montagu-Chelmsford report on constitutional reforms, published in June of 1918.

A special session of the All-India Congress was held in Bombay to consider the proposals, and curious proposals they were. By way of experiment, partial self-government was recommended for the provinces: the principle of dyarchy, it was termed. Certain affairs would be placed under the jurisdiction of a "cabinet" of Indian ministers drawn from an elected legislature while other affairs, "reserved subjects," would remain under the control of the governor and his advisory executive council. To the British, this was a seemly introduction to responsible government in the subcontinent. To most Indian Nationalists, however, it was a paltry concession, far short of the expectations that had been raised by the original Montagu Declaration. Faced with this situation, the Congress demanded "self-government within the Empire" immediately. It asserted that India was at that very moment ready for responsible government, and demanded the abandonment of the concept of dyarchy, which really would have left the central government and most vital provincial matters under the exclusive jurisdiction of the British. The Congress also demanded fiscal autonomy for India and a declaration of Indian rights.

This All-India Congress was hardly revolutionary, in any sense of the word. "God Save the King" was inscribed over the entrance to the pavilion, and the Congress tendered "its most loyal homage to His Gracious Majesty the King-Emperor." The constitutional old guard was hard in control of the Congress, and the habit of obeisance was too deeply ingrained in them to permit any action more drastic than polite criticism. Only a traumatic experience and a dramatic call to action could set the Congress on a new path.

The call was not long in coming. First came the Rowlatt Bills;

then came the Amritsar massacre. The massacre, indeed, grew indirectly from the Rowlatt Bills, for these bills led Gandhi to form the Satyagraha Society, whose members were pledged to civil disobedience; and he proclaimed April 6 as Satyagraha Day, a day of nation-wide mass meetings of protest.

The day of protest went off without incident, but on the 10th of April, in Amritsar, two Congress leaders were arrested, and within a matter of hours a mixed group of Europeans and Indians gathered to protest their being held. The police reserves were called out, the protest grew into a riot, a score of the demonstrators, including five Europeans, were killed.

The worst was still to come.

On the Hindu New Year's Day, April 13, despite a British ban on public meetings, the Congress party called for a demonstration in Amritsar, in a public park called Jallianwala Dagh, which was located almost in the heart of the city, enclosed on three sides by the high walls of adjoining houses. The only exit was about eight or ten feet wide—enough to permit only a few persons to pass at a time. An estimated 20,000 persons were in the park when a detachment of about 150 soldiers marched in through the one exit and attempted to disband the meeting. In such circumstances, a bloody and tragic end is all but inevitable. For those who like blame, it was clearly on the British: either the meeting should have been stopped before it started, or it should have been allowed to continue. Officers of His Majesty's regular troops did not think that way, however. In the melee, the order to fire was given, panic followed, and instead of halting, the firing increased. The senseless slaughter stopped only when the troops ran out of ammunition, and by then, as a Royal Commission of Inquiry later found, 379 had been killed and more than 1,200 wounded or injured.

Anglo-Indian relationships were exacerbated beyond all mending when Sir Michael O'Dwyer, governor of the Punjab, voiced his approval of the handling of the situation. He was determined to "teach the natives a lesson," he said, and he continued to rule with an iron hand. Nationalist leaders were jailed, public floggings were common; Indians were forced to get down on all fours and crawl to pass the end of a lane where a British woman medical missionary had been assaulted during the riots.

Rage and hatred burned through all of India. The park of Jallianwala Dagh became a shrine, and April 13 became a day of mourning. The Amritsar tragedy, one British historian wrote, was "a turning point in Indo-British relations almost as important as the Mutiny of 1857 because of the assumption, implied in the behavior of responsible Englishmen and in their evidence before the Hunter Commission that Indians could and should be treated as an inferior race." A former member of the Indian Civil Service went on record that "from now onward the whole situation was changed. Government had been carried on with consent—usually apathetic and half-hearted but still consent—of the governed. That consent was now changed to active mistrust."

A man on whom the incident had a most profound effect was Jawaharlal Nehru, then not quite twenty-nine years old. Life and circumstance were always good to Jawaharlal Nehru. He had been born into the Kashmiri Brahmin world, the most aristocratic subcaste of the Hindu social system, and he was well aware of his background. (He is supposed to have commented, years later, in a fit of pique at Winston Churchill, that "his ancestors were dressed in the skins of wild animals, roaming the forests of England and painting themselves with woad when mine were dressed in silk, writing books and painting pictures.") His father was a barrister, which in itself in that Edwardian age insured wealth and at least a minimum of sophistication, and since Nehru was an only son, he was the focus of family attention. He was denied nothing. There were the private tutors, then off to England to follow in his father's footsteps—Harrow, Cambridge, the Inner Temple. When he returned to India to enter politics (just as his father did to become a member of the nationalist movement), he followed in his father's footsteps, attending the Congress session in Bombay with Motilal Nehru, both of them, in the words of a not-too-admiring colleague, leaving no doubt "that they attended the meeting with a certain air of condescension." But the younger Nehru was of more fiery stuff than his father. Young Nehru participated in the Home Rule League demonstrations of 1917, he joined Gandhi's Satyagraha Society, and in time he would become Gandhi's disciple.

"My growth to public prominence, you know, was not by sharp

stages," Nehru reflected years later. "It was, rather, a steady development over a long period of time. And if I may say so, I began at a fairly high level." Of his first impressions of Gandhi, Nehru said: "All of us admire him for his heroic fight in South Africa, but he seemed very different and distant and unpolitical to many of us." This may have been due to the difference between Gandhi's fanatical simplicity and Nehru's instinct for aristocracy—although Nehru was able to say, when he heard of the formation of Gandhi's Satyagraha Society, that his feeling was one "of tremendous relief. Here at last was a way out of the tangle, a method of action which was straight and open and possibly effective. I was afire with enthusiasm and wanted to join immediately. I hardly thought of the consequences—law-breaking, jail-going, etc.—and if I thought of them I did not care."

If Nehru did not care, his father did. Motilal Nehru was very much a member of the establishment. He did not believe in non-cooperation, active or passive, and he thought his son, now a grown man of almost thirty, was a fool for considering going to jail. Once, in a rage, he ordered his son out of the house, an extreme step against an only son.

Nehru himself was not having an easy time. "For many days there was this mental conflict," he wrote. "Night after night I wandered out alone, tortured in mind and trying to grope my way out." At length, after months, there was a reconciliation between father and son. In part, it was due to the persuasiveness with which Gandhi argued his theories with Motilal Nehru. "It was a tremendous struggle," Jawaharlal Nehru wrote, "for [my father] to uproot himself and to fit himself into this new environment. . . . It was perhaps a triangle, Mr. Gandhi, my father, and myself, each influencing the other to some extent. But principally, I should imagine, it was Gandhi's amazing capacity to tone down the opposition by his friendly approach. Secondly, our closer association brought out that Gandhi was not only a very big man and a very fine man but also an effective man . . . [and] my father was forced to think because of my own reaction. I was his only son; he was much interested in me."

The Amritsar massacre also marked a major turning point in Nehru's life, a particularly bitter pill for him to swallow since, unlike Gandhi, the seven years he had spent in England had filled him with a deep admiration for the British concepts of tolerance and justice. Nehru was not at Amritsar; of this enormously important emotional experience he was to write, "helplessly and impotently, we who were outside waited for scraps of news, and bitterness filled our hearts. . . . I realized then, more vividly than I had ever done before, how brutal and immoral imperialism was and how it had eaten into the souls of the British upper classes."

It was this disillusion and bitterness that made Nehru a Nationalist.

At the end of 1919 the annual meeting of the Congress was held at Amritsar, a gesture of defiance to the British. Motilal Nehru presided, but Gandhi was slowly moving toward the fore. The measure of the man who was to see India's independence may be found in the words he used when he spoke to the delegates about the slaughter that had been committed at that place: "The government went mad at the time; we also went mad at the time. I say, do not return madness with madness, but return madness with sanity and the whole situation will be yours."

# VI

# NEITHER WAR NOR PEACE

> Dream after dream ensues,
> And still they dream that they
> shall succeed;
> And still are disappointed.
>
> COWPER

AS IN INDIA, WHERE in 1918 there was the beginning of the revolt that would eventually make her free, in Africa there were the first faint stirrings of independence. Almost two generations and another world war later would come the splintering of the continent into some two-score states.

When World War I broke out, the only independent nations in Africa were Liberia in the west and Ethiopia in the east; the remaining areas were national prizes of the nineteenth-century scramble for colonies by the European powers—the British, Germans, and French, and to a lesser extent by the Italians, Belgians, and Portugese. When the war broke out, the governor of German East Africa, Heinrich Schnee, was very much against letting the war move to Africa. "The prestige of the white man is at stake," he said. "If the natives learn that they can overcome the white man in battle, it will give them ideas that will be dangerous for the future of all Europeans in Africa."

General Paul von Lettow-Vorbeck, commander of the German military forces in East Africa—3,000 whites and 11,000 blacks—was one of the remarkable leaders of World War I. Although outnumbered almost two-to-one by a mixed bag of 27,350 British, South African, Indian, and African soldiers, he was the clear victor when the war ended. He endlessly maneuvered his men so that the British had no rest, forcing them to keep a force of some three divisions fighting in Africa rather than in Europe. And von Lettow-Vorbeck may unwittingly have sown the seeds of independence in the minds of the black men who served with him. He may have started off with the thought, common to Europeans in Africa, that the lowest white man was more valuable than the best black man, that the Africans were little more advanced than the apes of the jungles, that black soldiers fought only under the spur of the lash, but soon he was addressing his troops, black and white alike, as "we Africans" and was saying, "Here in Africa we are all equal, the better man will always outwit his inferior and the color of his skin does not matter. . . . The feeling of comradeship which our askaris feel for us Germans and we for them . . . led," according to von Lettow-Vorbeck "to a curious incident. After climbing Kasigao Mountain by night among rocks and thorn bushes, an askari noticed that Lieutenant von Ruckteschell was bleeding from a scratch on his face. He at once took his sock, which he had probably not changed for six days, and wiped the 'bwana lieutenant's' face with it, anticipating the somewhat surprised question with the remark: 'That is a custom; one only does it for one's friends.' "

After the war, Germany's colonies were divided among the British and the French for administration. At this time a Pan-African movement, headed by W. E. B. DuBois, began to emerge on the scene. Born in Great Barrington, Massachusetts, DuBois was the first American Negro Ph.D. from Harvard and was a founder of the National Association for the Advancement of Colored People in 1909. While serving as an observer at the Versailles Peace Conference in 1919, DuBois called a Pan-African Congress in Paris. (In later life he would join the Communist party and spend his last years as a citizen of Ghana; he died in Africa in 1963.) The Pan-African Congress, financed by the NAACP, was designed to give Negroes around the world a sense of identity with Africa. Wilson's Fourteen Points had spoken of the self-determination of small nations—why not for the nations of Africa? But the congress was doomed to disappointment, as were the congresses of 1921, 1923, and 1927. National self-determination would not have meaning in Africa until another war and a generation later. One tiny step forward was taken, however, with the establishment of the mandate system which provided for the governing of colonies that had belonged to the defeated powers by number states of the League of Nations (especially Britain and France).

It is ironic that even with almost total independence today, many of the systems introduced by the colonial powers are still being used in Africa. Two important characteristics strengthened the colonial system. The first was that government was by an all-powerful executive assisted by an elite corps of specialists. (In many of the new African states today the new rulers use the same system to maintain their power. In some cases, the "elite specialists" are the same whites who were there before independence.) The second strength was that the chief colonial executive dominated the economic as well as the political structure—a form of enlightened dictatorship.

Another continent that underwent great change as a result of the war, though not so much as others, was Latin America. Throughout most of the war, Latin America maintained a more or less effective neutrality, but after the United States entered the war, eight Latin American states also went to war, in various ways. While Brazil was the only South American country actually to declare war, seven Central American nations—Costa Rica, Cuba, Guatemala, Haiti, Honduras, Nicaragua, and Panama—were de facto belligerents. Five countries severed diplomatic relations with Germany: Bolivia, the Dominican Republic, Ecuador, Peru, and Uruguay. Remaining neutral throughout the war were Argentina, Chile, Colombia, Mexico, Paraguay, El Salvador, and Venezuela. The Latin American countries that went to war against the Central Powers, or severed relations with them, did so in great part because of their admiration of Wilson's utopian dreams, because they believed that the Central Powers had violated basic principles of international law, and because they felt a sense of cultural and ideological identity with the Allies.

The Latin American nations did not play a major role in the actual fighting, but their participation in the war moved them from the periphery of international politics toward its center. Eleven of these nations sent official delegations to the Paris Peace Conference and signed the Treaty of Versailles. Seventeen of them—all except Mexico, the Dominican Republic, and Ecuador—became members of the League of Nations, forming a substantial 36 percent of its total membership, and Brazil was given an interim seat on the council.

This was the great change that the war brought to Latin America—her emergence onto the world scene. For generations she had been both protected and deformed by the Monroe Doctrine. It was true that under this doctrine she had been saved from the depredations—military, political, and economic—that the European powers had inflicted on other continents, but she had been under the dominance, largely economic, of the United States. With her emergence onto the world stage at the end of World War I, all this began to change, and the doctrine of the early nineteenth-century hero, Simon Bolivar, that envisioned a United Latin America becoming a great force in the world rivaling the power of France or Great Britain, gained new currency.

If, for Europeans, the years before 1914 had been halcyon years of pleasure and ease, still to be viewed in the delicious and dreaming half light of the early Impressionists, for Americans those years had been a time of lusty young growth—and of innocence. True, it was also for America a time of turbulence, a time when the robber barons were still carving their private fortunes out of a free land, a time of the beginnings of the industrial slums and of bloody battles with the labor unions. It was also the last time of innocence.

For America, World War I was minor compared to the Civil War, but in retrospect, even despite the nation's failure to join the League of Nations, it was the war that brought the nation into the world. Not many Americans realized it. The automobile had not yet taken control of the country. Delivery men—the man who brought the ice for the icebox in these days before the electric refrigerator, the milkman, the coal men with coal for the furnace and the kitchen stove and the fireplace in the living room —delivered their goods in horse-drawn carts; not until the twenties would the auto displace the horse. It was still possible to ride a bicycle, or a horse, or even walk along a suburban road without being run down or questioned by the police; travel was by train or—between cities—by that delicious and unique invention, the interurban trolley. Of the millions of people in the United States then, it is doubtful if one in a thousand had ever crossed the ocean or had ever seen an airplane at close range. Mass-produced radio had not yet arrived, television was still a textbook theory, and not everyone had a telephone. Most Americans had never been two hundred miles from where they lived. It is possible now to discern the entry of America as a nation into the world, but it was then a barely perceptible change; the newspapers concentrated on the dangers of the European revolutions. On November 11, *The New York Times* found anarchy second in importance only to the end of fighting itself: ARMISTICE SIGNED, END OF THE WAR! read the *Times* headline. BERLIN SEIZED BY REVOLUTIONISTS, NEW CHANCELLOR BEGS FOR ORDER, OUSTED KAISER FLEES TO HOLLAND.

The kind of capitalism that had developed in America since the end of the Civil War was quite different from the capitalism that developed in Europe and tended to make the United States more conservative. The Industrial Revolution in Europe had brought the concept of capitalism to a society already long established and therefore competent to assimilate foreign notions into the body politic. The United States was in theory a classless society, one in which men could still homestead land, a violent society that had established its boundaries by the rifle and the six-gun. It was highly conservative and unwilling to consider any foreign notions. By the time of World War I it had already established its conservatism; even its trade unionism under men like Samuel Gompers and his successors William Green and George Meany was essentially conservative.

Still high among America's heroes were the "robber barons" (who were not to fall into disrepute, as far as the general culture went, until the Depression) like Edward H. Harriman ("He made one million a month the last twelve years of his life," wrote one magazine), John D. Rockefeller, Henry Ford, and John Hays Hammond.

John Dewey might be writing in *The New Republic* about "creative industry" and spreading another of his iconoclastic notions, but most of the nation's newspapers and magazines—since they themselves were (and are) businesses and, by the laws of the economic system in which they operate, must show a profit to continue to operate—wrote and worried about anarchism, socialism, bolshevism, and communism. At this place in America's history, that was the order in which they were feared. America had had its taste of anarchy: the International Workers of the World —the Wobblies—had talked of anarchy, and anarchists were held responsible in some quarters for the Los Angeles *Times* explosion in 1910, when twenty-one people were killed, for the bombing of the Preparedness Day Parade in San Francisco in July of 1916 in which ten were killed and the Black Tom explosion in Jersey City a week later, and for the Wall Street explosion of 1920. On the other hand, socialism was known through the activities of Eugene Victor Debs, for example, and it was the Second International of the International Socialist Bureau that had brought together, in Brussels in 1914, five men who would later head the governments of their respective countries—Lenin from Russia, Ebert from Germany, MacDonald of England, Branting of Sweden, and Stauning of Denmark.

Lincoln Steffens was at the height of his fame, although already tired of "muck-raking" and turning to his admiration of revolutions ("I would like to spend the evening of my life," he wrote, "watching the morning of a new world") that took him to Mexico for the revolutions that convulsed that land for the decade that began in 1911, then to Russia, and to Italy in 1923. At Harvard there were the Single Tax and the Anarchist Clubs, the Harvard Men's Club for Women's Suffrage, and the Socialist Club where Walter Lippmann spoke and John Reed (later to go to Russia and to write *Ten Days That Shook the World*) listened, but Harvard men have always by and large been emotional and romantic.

*The New York Times,* dealing with the facts of the real world, was telling of the wild anarchy in Austria on the first of November 1918 and of panic in the German provinces along the Rhine on rumors that the cities of Cologne and Coblentz were to be occupied by the Allies. The *Times* also reported that "the long-deferred report of Charles E. Hughes on American aircraft production . . . failed to reveal or charge glaring defalcations and peculations . . . and brings charges principally against Col. E. A. Deeds of the Aircraft Administration largely for lack of force." Alfred E. Smith was campaigning for governor of New York; William H. Taft and Theodore Roosevelt were urging the voters to vote Republican; theater magnate A. Paul Keith (who had helped give the nation vaudeville) died, and to prove that there always was an adman, one store proclaimed, "The Peace We Offer Is Peace of Mind If You Buy Your Clothes in a Brill Store."

In a New York magazine, the Reverend Robert Davis of the Englewood, New Jersey, Red Cross Mission to France, wrote:

> To the Women of America from American Men in France. It is a still Sunday afternoon in a still clean valley, the first Sunday of the first Expeditionary Force in their permanent camp. The church bells are ringing back home, in the white churches of the villages, in the stone churches on city corners, and you are entering your places, where we have in other times sat beside you—where we, as little boys, rested our sleepy heads on your comfortable laps, you mothers—where we stood beside you and held your singing prayer books when we were first married, you wives—where we watched you shyly as you bowed during prayer, you girls of golden hopes. . . .
>
> It is sweet and glorious to die, for our country is no longer a shibboleth but a vital truth pulsating through the veins of young America.

The same magazine also pointed out the dangerous "socialistic tendency" in the government inherent in Wilson's decision to put the railroads under government control and asked whether the government control would continue after the war, as seemed likely in Britain. (The magazine also reported that railroad stocks "soared" on the stock exchange after Wilson announced that the government would guarantee returns to the bond and stock holders of an average of the previous three years, which meant that they could not lose as long as the government held the roads.) The almost unlimited capacity of the human establishment to carry on an infinite number of activities at the same time—and the repetitiveness of human history—is found in those days of fifty years ago. There were the clichés of "brave, bleeding Serbia" and "devastated Belgium," the "heroic new nation" born of the war—Czechoslovakia—"four races whose unquenchable idealism and indomitable spirit have saved for the world the Czecho-Slovak nation, the Moravians, the Silesians, the Slovenes, and the Bohemians." There was fuel rationing (the winters of 1918 were especially bitter; on New Year's Day the director-general of the Railroad Administration was taking "radical steps" to unsnarl the transportation lines of the East where frozen engines were halting trains hauling coal to the below-zero states of the Northeast; factories were closed for lack of fuel; the coroner in New York City reported twelve deaths due to the cold); Elbert H. Gary was president of United States Steel; Lucius Boomer was managing director of the McAlpin Hotel; *Leslie's Illustrated Weekly* was going great guns, but the easy, leisurely life of an earlier age was ending—Delmonico's went into receivership.

A shuttle train subway service was opened in New York City between Grand Central Station and Times Square; but the crush was so great that it had to be closed. (It was reopened, without fanfare, six weeks later.) In Brooklyn occurred the worst subway wreck in American—and possibly world—history. A strike by motormen started the morning of November 2 on the lines of the Brooklyn Rapid Transit Company, and the trains were being run by some supervisors who were also qualified as motormen. A Brighton Beach train was running late and either to make up time (earlier it had taken a wrong track because of a switching mistake and had had to back up) or because it went out of control —to this day, no one knows—it was doing an estimated seventy miles an hour when it hit the curve in the Old Malbone Street tunnel in Brooklyn. Even allowing for exaggeration (fifty miles an hour was—and is—pretty fast for a subway train), the train was far over the speed limit and didn't make the turn. When the first car went off the tracks, the others telescoped into each other, and almost one hundred persons were killed as the wooden coaches splintered into carnage.

The United States underwent changes to the fabric of living that would not become apparent for years to come. For the first time, a number of forces were at work that were to change the world for the American Negro. First, the phrase "to make the world safe for democracy" had become part of the legend of the world; a war had been fought for this. No longer a phrase in a high-school civics book, it was an actuality that was part of real life. To increase the intensity of the understanding of this, some 400,000 Negroes had been drafted in World War I, and most of them found themselves thoroughly discriminated against both in the barracks and in the cities where they went for recreation. But about half of the Negroes who were drafted were sent overseas, where they found themselves treated more like heroes, or at least like victorious warriors. When they returned to the United States, of course, all that changed; but they had had the experience of respect. The war had also changed the economic and industrial look of the nation itself. World War I had been the first of the total wars; while its impact had not been felt in the United States as it had been in France or England, still it had drawn masses of young men—and young women—from the rural and agricultural districts of the country to the factories of the industrial areas. Too, the businessman and banker might have cried "socialism" about the way in which the government took control of shipping on land and on sea, and established controls over production and consumption, but the government had no socialism at all in its soul; the moment that the war was over the controls were withdrawn, the laissez-faire system returned. So the returning soldiers and sailors and the workers in the munitions plants and the war factories were thrown onto the labor market at once, while there was comparatively little of the pent-up demand for consumer goods that was to so change the picture after World War II.

The result was inevitable. Only months after the war was over, a depression began to build up in the United States—one that was to sweep the rest of the world as well—and one that was to have the additional misfortune of bringing whites and Negroes into bitter and bloody conflict. One of the nation's worst waves of lynching swept the South, race riots tore apart the North. It was more than simply the depression, the first outright competition for factory jobs: it was part of the whole turbulent surge of change that was taking place on the American scene.

After the Civil War, for example—the last of the heroic wars—returning veterans were the folk idols of their towns. Not so after World War I. The war had really been too short for America; it had been more of a lark, a vacation from the humdrum of civilian life. Much more lay beneath the turbulence. It was not simply that the returning veterans had seen parts of the world with patterns of society utterly alien, different from what they had known whether they came from the industrial North or the farmlands of the Midwest or the caste-set South; it was that the

America they were returning to was in the throes of the change from an agricultural nation to an industrial one, where the social patterns of the small towns and the economics of the small individual farmer were breaking up before their eyes.

In this time of change a Negro movement, the Universal Negro Improvement Association, came into being and quickly attracted many followers. Its founder, Marcus Garvey, was a West Indian Negro, one of that breed that almost from childhood has visions of leading the black man out of bondage and into his own birthright. Garvey wanted nothing to do with the white man or with any Negro—including the leadership of the NAACP, from DuBois on down—who was willing to deal with the white man. Garvey was one of the very earliest advocates of black power; to him, the future of his race lay with the *really* black men; he harkened back to the glory of the ages and argued that Jesus Christ himself had been black.

"Was not the Negro a power, was he not great once?" Garvey demanded. "Yes, honest students can recall the day when Egypt, Ethiopia, and Timbuctoo towered in their civilizations, towered above Europe, towered above Asia. When Europe was inhabited by a race of cannibals, a race of savages, naked men, heathens and pagans, Africa was peopled with a race of cultured black men who were masters in art, science, and literature; men who were cultured and refined; men who, it was said, were like the gods. Even the great poets of old sang in beautiful sonnets of the delight it afforded the gods to be in companionship with the Ethiopians. Why, then, should we lose hope? Black men, you were once great; you shall be great again. Lose not courage, lose not faith, go forward."

In a space of three years, Garvey was able to create a black fraternal order in the United States of several million members whose aim was to return to Africa; an "Empire of Africa" was formally announced, which Garvey was to head and which had created a nobility of its own that included the Dukes of Niger and Uganda, which was arguing its cause with Liberia, Ethiopia, and the League of Nations.

Garvey's flaw in creating his association was not so much organizational as fiscal.

Indeed, his organization itself was formidable: its military and paramilitary arms included the Black Eagle Flying Corps, the Universal Black Cross Nurses, the Universal African Legion, and the Universal African Motor Corps. He also built a business empire that included printing plants, retail stores, hotels and restaurants, and a newspaper, the *Negro World*. It was in creating a shipping line, the Black Star line, to move his people back to Africa, that Garvey ran afoul of the Federal government. He had been able to raise more money in less time than any other Negro leader—and than most white leaders—but now he was convicted of using the mails to defraud, served two years in a Federal penitentiary, and was deported as an undesirable alien.

Gunnar Myrdal cites Garvey as one of the classic examples of the "American dilemma," that only a movement appealing to black chauvinism can have a broad appeal for the American Negro, yet exactly such an appeal will alienate white middle-class support for the movement, without which success is all but impossible.

Communications were changing, and so was mobility.

The mass-circulation newspaper, the telephone, and the automobile had come into their own in the first quarter of the century. It was not so much, as some social critics have said, that the machine was taking over the world as that the machine was remaking the mind of man. No longer was it accepted that the news in a newspaper should be days or even weeks late; the news had to be immediate, and immediacy has its own role to play with the human creature. During the Civil War, or the Boer War or the Boxer Rebellion, the news came late, days after the action, and by then all might have changed. But now, with the telegraph and the telephone, the stories of the slaughter at Cambrai were on the breakfast table the next morning. The stories of race riots, the lynchings, and the hangings were there. And the auto—with the road system it forced to be built—could salvage you from doom if doom looked imminent.

The Edwardian age had taken over from the Victorian, and if it is unarguable that the relations between the sexes never alter, only the customs and usages of the presex rituals, the war itself forced the big change. There was the mere physical fact that there were more women, and more women available; the office and the factory were drawing them from the home. There was the charging excitement of the war itself, always more evanescent on the home front. There was more an obsession with death, itself a correlation of sex. Life in the trenches of France was hardly honored—it was the cheapest commodity about. The teachings of the various religions that man is the image of God, that man is somehow greater than other animals, possessed of a soul that insures his continued existence in an after world, were attacked from all sides; it followed then that the wages of sin were likely to be fun more than anything else. Beyond the argument of the ambitious young lover that tomorrow he might die lay the argument of sophists that more and more babies were needed to make up for the slaughter of the war and the statement of conservative members of Parliament that no stigma should be attached to "the mothers of our soldiers' children" or to the children themselves; illegitimate children accounted for 30 percent more of the births in England at the end of the war.

Once the war was over, the automobile—more specifically the cheap automobile—carried on this age of freedom. From the twenties on, the auto was not only the world's most ubiquitous place of assignation but also the great leveler, the great maker of social equality. In a way it became a symbol of sex and a symbol of power. On the installment plan, the weakling could buy a car that would make him the equal of Atlas, transforming him from a ninety-seven-pound nothing by the mere signing of a credit company form. The equalizing power of the auto went deeper than that, for who could tell whether the man who signed the installment form, once away from his home, was rich man, poor man, beggar man, thief? Here was the instrument that would allow the poor man to see America on his vacation on equal terms with the very rich, that would allow the depression-bankrupt tenant farmers to get to California, that would allow the bootlegger to make a success of his trade. It let the ordinary man feel that he was as good as the best—that if there were a hierarchy of nobility in the United States, he would be a member of it.

There were those cynics who ascribed the slow decay of the red-light districts to the increasing use of the automobile, though there were those who ascribed it to suffragism. Skirts, which had been regarded as "short" when they were ankle-length in 1914, were knee-length or less by the early twenties; the silk stocking appeared as the corset and the petticoat vanished; the Lucky Strike cigarette people were advertising: "And now, women may enjoy a companionable smoke with their husbands and brothers—at the same time slenderizing in a sensible manner . . . Reach for a Lucky instead of a sweet."

The moral revolution, as well as the political, the economic, and the social, was in full swing. And as always after a really cataclysmic war, the defeated felt the moral impact the worst. The guidebooks of the cities like Hamburg and Berlin, being sold openly back then, might give pause even to an underground filmmaker of today. The author Stefan Sweig talked of the Berlin of that day: "I have a pretty thorough knowledge of history, but never to my recollection had it produced such madness in such gigantic proportions. . . . Even the Rome of Suetonius had never known such madness as the pervert balls at Berlin. . . . But the most revolting thing about this pathetic eroticism was its spuriousness. . . . Whoever lived through these apocalyptic months, these years, disgusted and embittered, sensed the coming of the horrible reaction."

Strangely, it was the people at home, the ones who had not seen the blood of the battlefield or suffered defeat in arms, who gave themselves most thoroughly to the perversions of the day. The soldiers who were still under arms and who, it would turn out, would be the ones to shape the years ahead, would come to be more bitter about their countrymen at home than they were against the enemy that had defeated them.

None of the things that were happening then were to prepare the world for what was really to come. The length of skirts, the slogans of cigarette makers, the nightclub shows and plays, are the amusements of a summer's day—they are not presumed to set the course of civilization. But onto the stage of the world, after Wilson came Harding. After Nicholas came Stalin. After Wilhelm, Hitler. After Umberto, Mussolini.

In the United States, after the winter of the world, all was returning to normal. In Washington, the Senate was beginning debates on the "League for Peace." Republican Senator Poindexter of Washington said that joining any such organization would necessitate rewriting the Constitution and would abrogate the Monroe Doctrine. Republican Senator Penrose of Pennsylvania said that in view of their victory the Republicans would write the tax bill for 1920 and that their plans included new protective tariffs. Professor Tomas G. Masaryk, president of the new Republic of Czechoslovakia, had dinner at Delmonico's before sailing back to Prague. Gimbel's was advertising its Thanksgiving sales. Al Jolson was appearing in *Sinbad* and Charlie Chaplin in *Shoulder Arms*. Jack Dempsey fought Joe Bonds. Alice Brady was in *Forever After* and Jane Cowl in *The Crowded Hour*.

The forces that had won the war and that had been defeated by the war were now defined. Socialism, even though it was to take another twenty years to make clear, had been defeated, even in Russia; monarchism had lost and imperialism was beginning to be challenged on all sides. Democracy and the theory of democracy would be able to survive in the most favored nations; the way had been paved for the dictator. The universities, which for the first time had supported a war along nationalist lines, and the organized religions which had followed the same course, were on the brim of their long decline. The power elite that had been established by the Industrial Revolution—the banker, the manufacturer, the industrialist—had been reaffirmed, and along with it, an extension that included the scientist who could invent new weapons of great destructiveness and the technician who could devise methods of putting them into mass production.

Against this, Woodrow Wilson's sweet dream of a world without war seemed a dream indeed.

In Times Square, *The New York Times* began to offer its "War Volumes" at bargain prices.

And so the excitement of America's first venture into the world of planet-round conflict and diplomacy seemed over. It is trite now to say that the nation retreated into isolationism—it did, but patterns had been broken that would not be re-mended in a half century of years. For all the defeats that Wilson had suffered, his vain but glorious crusade for the League of Nations had burned a scar in the American consciousness that was eventually to lead, not only to American support for the United Nations, but for the establishment of the United Nations headquarters on American soil. And it requires no great feat of logic to see that Wilson's principle of the self-determination of small countries is the principle upon which the entire American dialectic for being in South Vietnam is premised. To mention only one other vastly important development clearly recognizable with twenty-twenty hindsight, it was the initial American reaction to the Russian Revolution of 1917 that was to color the American attitude to Russia even until today. Franklin D. Roosevelt, it was true, was able to obtain diplomatic recognition of Russia, and there have been periods of thaw in the relationship since World War II, but the basic American distrust of any form of radicalism is never very far from the political surface.

# BIBLIOGRAPHY

# BIBLIOGRAPHY


Antonius, G. *The Arab Awakening.* Beirut: Khayatas, 1939.

Armeson, R. *Total Warfare and Compulsory Labor; A Study of the Military-Industrial Complex in Germany During World War I.* Hague: Nijhoff, 1964.

Armstrong, E. *Crisis of Quebec, 1914–18.* New York: Columbia, 1937.

Army Times. *The Yanks are Coming.* New York: Putnam, 1960.

Aston, Sir George Grey. *Biography of Marshal Foch.* New York: Macmillan, 1929.

Barber, Frederick. *The Horror of It.* New York: Brewer, Warren & Putnam, 1932.

Barnett, Correlli. *Swordbearers: Supreme Command in World War I.* New York: Morrow, 1964.

Beaverbrook, William. *Men and Power, 1917–18.* New York: Duell, Sloan & Pearce, 1957.

Bourne, Randolph. *War and the Intellectuals.* New York: Harper, 1964.

Bruun, Geoffrey. *Clemenceau.* Connecticut: Archon, 1962.

Buchan, John. *The People's King, George V.* Boston: Houghton Mifflin, 1935.

Bugnet, Charles. *Foch Speaks.* New York: Dial Press, 1929.

Bunyan, James. *Intervention, Civil War, and Communism in Russia, April–December 1918; Documents and Materials.* Baltimore: Johns Hopkins, 1936.

Bykov, Davel. *The Last Days of Tsar Nicholas.* New York: International, 1934.

Chamberlin, William. *Soviet Russia.* Boston: Little, Brown, 1930.

Chase, Stuart. *The Most Probable World.* New York: Harper & Row.

Churchill, Winston S. *Great Contemporaries.* London: Butterworth, 1937.

———. *Shall We Commit Suicide?*
———. *The World Crisis.* 6 volumes. New York: Scribner's 1923–31.
Clemenceau, Georges. *Grandeur and Misery of Victory.* New York: Harcourt, Brace, 1930.
Commaerts, E. *Albert of Belgium.* New York: Macmillan, 1935.
Dalin, E. *French and German Public Opinion.*
Edwards, M. *Stresemann and the Greater Germany.* New York: Bookman, 1963.
Farbman, Michael. *Russia and the Struggle for Power.* London: Allen & Unwin, 1918.
Fifield, R. *Woodrow Wilson and the Far East.* Connecticut: Archon, 1965.
Fischer, Fritz. *Germany's Aims in the First World War.* New York: Norton, 1967.
Foch, Ferdinand. *Memories of Marshal Foch.* New York: Doubleday, Doran, 1931.
Fredericks, Pierce. *The Great Adventure; America in the First World War.* New York: Dutton, 1960.
Gallatin, Albert. *Art and the Great War.* New York: Dutton, 1919.
Gelfand, Lawrence. *The Inquiry; American Preparations for Peace, 1917–19.* New Haven: Yale, 1963.
George V. *The King to His People; Speeches and Messages Delivered Between July 1911 and May 1935.* London: Williams and Northgate, 1935.
Gerard, J. W. *Face to Face with Kaiserism.* New York: Doran, 1918.
Germains, V. *The Tragedy of Winston Churchill.* London: Hurst & Blackett, 1931.
Gibbs, Philip. *Now It Can Be Told.* New York: Harper, 1920.
*Harper's Pictorial Library of the World War.* New York: Harper, 1921.
Harrison, Marguerite. *Asia Reborn.* New York: Harper, 1928.
Hindenburg, Paul von. *Out of My Life.* New York: Harper, 1921.
Hitler, Adolf. *Mein Kampf.* New York: Stackpole Sons, 1939.
Hoover, Herbert. *An American Epic.* Chicago: Regnery, 1959–61.
———. *America's First Crusade.* New York: Scribner's, 1942.

———. *Memoirs.* 3 volumes. New York: Macmillan, 1951–52.

———. *Ordeal of Woodrow Wilson.* New York: McGraw-Hill, 1958.

———. *Since the Armistice.* Washington: Chamber of Commerce, 1919.

———. *We Cannot Fiddle While Rome Burns.* New York: League to Enforce Peace, 1919.

House, Edward. *The Intimate Papers of Colonel House.* Ed. by Charles Seymour. 4 volumes. Boston: Houghton Mifflin, 1926–28.

Hunter, Thomas. *Marshal Foch, A Study in Leadership.*

Kennan, George F. "The Russian Revolution." *Outlook.* New York: 1918. Volume 119, pages 379–98.

———. *Soviet-American Relations, 1917–1920.* 2 volumes. Volume 1 Russia Leaves the War. 1956; volume 2 Decision to Intervene. 1958. New Jersey: Princeton.

Kerenski, Alexander. *The Catastrophe.* New York: Appleton, 1927.

King, Jere. *Foch Versus Clemenceau.* Cambridge: Harvard, 1960.

Komarnicki, T. *Rebirth of the Polish Republic.* London: Heinemann, 1957.

Langsam, Walter. *The World Since 1914.* New York: Macmillan, 1936.

Lawrence, T. E. *Revolt in the Desert.* New York: Doran, 1927.

———. *Seven Pillars of Wisdom.* New York: Doubleday, 1935.

Lenin, Vladimir. *Collected Works.* London: Lawrence & Wishert, 1960.

Liddell, Hart B. *Colonel Lawrence.* New York: Dodd, Mead, 1934.

———. *The Red Army.* New York: Harcourt, Brace, 1956.

Lippmann, Walter. *The Political Scene: An Essay on the Victory of 1918.* New York: Holt, 1919.

Lloyd, George David. *British War Aims* (statement of 1.5.18.). New York: Doran, 1918.

———. *Great Crusade.* New York: Doran, 1918.

———. *Is It Peace?* London: Hodder & Stoughton, 1923.

———. *Memoirs of the Peace Conference.* New Haven: Yale, 1939.

———. *Lloyd George's Message: Looking Forward.* London: National War Aims Committee, 1918.

———. *Prime Minister on the Peace Treaty*. London: Smith, 1919.
———. *War Memoirs of Lloyd George*. 6 volumes. London: Nicholson & Watson, 1933–36.
———. *When the War Will End* (statement of 6.29.17). London: Hayman, Christy & Hilly, 1917.
———. *The Worst is Over* (statement of 9.12.18). London: Hodder, 1918.
Martin, Laurence W. *Peace Without Victory*. New Haven: Yale, 1958.
Marwick, A. *The Deluge: British Society and World War I*. Boston: Little, Brown, 1966.
Masaryk, Tomas. *The Making of a State: Memories and Observations, 1914–18*. New York: Stokes, 1927.
Masefield, John. *The War and the Future*. New York: Macmillan, 1918.
Millard, T. F. *Democracy and the Eastern Question*. New York: Century, 1919.
Mitchell, William. *Memoirs of World War I*. New York: Random House, 1960.
Mock, J. R. *Words That Won the War: The Story of the Committee on Public Information, 1917–19*. New Jersey: Princeton University, 1939.
Muller, George von. *The Kaiser and His Court*. London: MacDonald, 1961.
Nicholson, Harold. *Peacemaking 1919*.
Pares, Sir Bernard. *A History of Russia*. New York: Knopf, 1953.
Pershing, J. J. *General Pershing's Story of the American Army in France*. New York: Herzig & McLean, 1919.
———. *My Experiences in the World War*. New York: Stokes, 1931.
Pfeifer, Wilhelm. *War and the German Mind*. New York: Columbia, 1941.
Pitt, Barrie. *1918, The Last Act*. New York: Norton, 1962.
Pound, R. *Lost Generation of 1914*. New York: Coward-McCann, 1965.
Rauch, George von. *History of Soviet Russia*. New York: Praeger, 1964.

*The Red Archives.* Ed. by C. E. Vuliamy. London: Bles, 1929.

Reed, John. *Ten Days That Shook the World.* New York: Boni & Liveright, 1919.

Remarque, Erich M. *All Quiet on the Western Front.* Boston: Little, Brown, 1929.

Robinson, James Harvey. *The Last Decade of European History and the Great War.* Boston: Ginn, 1918.

Roosevelt, Theodore. *Works of Theodore Roosevelt.* 24 volumes. New York: Scribner's, 1923–26.

———. *Letters of Theodore Roosevelt.* Ed. by Etling Morison. 8 volumes. Cambridge: Harvard, 1951–54.

Ross, Edward A. *Russian-Bolshevik Revolution.* New York: Century, 1921.

Seton-Watson, Robert. *Masaryk in England.* New York: Cambridge University Press, 1943.

Seymour, Charles. *Woodrow Wilson and the World War.* New Haven: Yale University Press, 1921.

Shelton, Brenda. *President Wilson and the Russian Revolution.* Buffalo: University of Buffalo, 1957.

Shokokhov, M. A. *And Quiet Flows the Don.* New York: Knopf, 1934.

Sidebotham, Herbert. *England and Palestine.* London: Constable, 1918.

Simonds, F. *They Won the War.* New York: Harper, 1931.

Slosson, Preston W. *The Great Crusade and After, 1914–1928.* New York: Macmillan, 1931.

Smith, Gene. *When the Cheering Stopped; The Last Years of Woodrow Wilson.* New York: Morrow, 1964.

Sprague, L. *Suppression of Dissent During the Civil War and World War I.* Syracuse University, 1959.

Stalin, Joseph. Works. 13 volumes. Moscow: Foreign Languages Pub. House, 1952–55.

Stresemann, Gustav. *Essays and Speeches.* London: Butterworth, 1930.

———. *Gustav Stresemann: His Diaries, Letters and Papers.* 3 volumes. London: Macmillan, 1935–40.

Sun Yat-sen. *Memoirs of a Chinese Revolutionary.* London: Hutchinson, 1927.

Thompson, Donald. *From Czar to Kaiser, The Betrayal of Russia.* New York: Doubleday, Page, 1918.

Thorn, George. "Sidelights on the Psychology of the Russian Revolution from Dostoevsky." *Contemporary Review.* Volume 113, pp. 695–700.

Trask, David. *United States in the Supreme War Council.* Connecticut: Wesleyan University. 1961.

Trotsky, Leon. *My Life.* New York: Scribner's, 1930.

———. *History of the Russian Revolution to Brest-Litovsk.* London: Macmillan, 1919.

Trotsky, Leon. *The Russian Revolution.* Ed. by F. W. Dupee. New York: Doubleday, 1959.

———. *The Trotsky Papers, 1917–22.* Hague: Mouton, 1964.

Tuchman, Barbara. *The Guns of August.* New York: Macmillan, 1962.

Tyrkova, A. *From Liberty to Brest-Litovsk.* London: Macmillan, 1919.

Veblen, Thorstein. *Essays in Our Changing Order.* New York: Kelley Reprint, 1964.

Viereck, George. *Spreading Germs of Hate.* New York: Liveright, 1930.

Warth, Robert. *The Allies and the Russian Revolution from the Fall of the Monarchy to the Treaty of Brest-Litovsk.* North Carolina: Duke University Press.

Wells, H. G. *War and the Future.* London: Cassell, 1917.

Wheeler, W. R. *China and the World War.* London: Macmillan, 1919.

Wheeler-Bennett, John. *Brest-Litovsk, the Forgotten Peace, March 1918.* London: Macmillan, 1956.

———. *Wooden Titan: Hindenburg in 20 Years of German History.* Hamden: Archon Books, 1963.

Wilhelm II. *The Kaiser's Memoirs.*

Williams, Harold. "Russia and the Peace Conference." *Edinburgh Review.* Volume 229, pp. 271–289.

Wilson, Woodrow. *Public Papers.* 16 volumes. New York: Harper, 1925–27.

Zweig, Arnold. *The Case of Sergeant Grisha.* New York: Viking, 1928.

# INDEX

# INDEX

PACE UNIVERSITY LIBRARIES
MORTOLA STACKS D523.C315 1968
1918; year of crisis, year of change
3 5061 00115 6950